ONE FOR THE BOOKS

Also by John M. Daniel

PLAY MELANCHOLY BABY

THE WOMAN BY THE BRIDGE

THE LOVE STORY OF SUSHI AND SASHIMI

One for the Books

∽

Confessions of a Small-Press Publisher

JOHN M. DANIEL

Fithian Press
Santa Barbara 1997

Copyright © 1997 by John M. Daniel
All rights reserved
Printed in the United States of America

ISBN 1-56474-224-5

Published by Fithian Press
A division of Daniel and Daniel, Publishers, Inc.
Post Office Box 1525
Santa Barbara, CA 93102

Book design: Eric Larson

*To Neil Daniel, my teacher
and to Susan Daniel, my partner*

Contents

Introduction 9

Learning to Read and Write 13

Deadlines and No Dead Lines 39

Two for the Books 66

The Payoff 98

Introduction

When Susan and I go on vacation each year in Mexico, we enjoy meeting new people, but we dread the question that almost inevitably comes up: "What do you folks do?" Depending on how many drinks we've had, we might answer, "Read, snorkel, drink tequila," or "We stick pictures of our kids on the refrigerator, just like you," or "We're hired killers in the CIA/Mafia, but we're not allowed to discuss it. Buy you a drink?"

But eventually we have to admit, "We're book publishers." We hope that will be an end on it, but it never is. The next question is, "What kind of books do you publish?"

"Green books. Yellow ones. We did a couple of brown books this year...."

It's not that we don't love what we do. It's just that we do it nonstop, fifty weeks of the year. We spend nearly all our time together, and the business is always with us, whether we're at the office or at home or on the road. Even when we're in bed there's a good chance one of us is dreaming about the business. Or lying awake fretting.

So when we go on vacation, don't ask us, "How's business?" We don't know and we don't care. Publishing is the one thing we don't think about in Mexico. Not even in bed. Especially not even in bed.

Once someone finds out we're book publishers, whether we're on vacation or not, the conversation can go in one of two ways. If the someone's a writer (at least half the people we meet are writers eager to be authors), then the conversation can turn into a complicated dance that can ruin an evening. But if it's just a normal person (as opposed to a writer), then the next question we are invited to answer is, "How did you get into that line of work?"

We have our answers. Susan tells about having owned a bookstore with her mother on Balboa Island during the 1970s, and I mention the Radcliffe course and the Stanford University Press. But every time I hear that question, I'm tempted to reminisce about how my attraction to publishing really began and how it grew.

People we meet on vacation won't sit still while I tell my entire life story, and neither will the reader of these pages. As an editor who is offered dozens of memoirs and autobiographies every week, I know that most of them are of interest mainly to the writer. I expect this book is no exception. I've also noticed, though, that when a memoir does have any value for other people it focuses on one aspect of the writer's life, some area of interest that people care about.

I don't know how many people care about small-press publishing, but this memoir is for those few. Readers will not have to suffer through the details of my life except for where they touch on publishing (and to some extent writing, and to a lesser extent, bookselling). Friends, family, and former wives may be relieved or disappointed; but the general intelligent reader will no doubt be glad that I'm writing about something grander than myself.

ONE FOR THE BOOKS

CHAPTER ONE
Learning to Read and Write

I ONCE ASKED my son Morgan what he wanted to be when he grew up, and he said he'd like to be a professional BMX bicycle rider. Not bad. He may be that yet, although it's been a couple of decades since he said that.

I learned to ride a bicycle at the age of five, from a man named Seth Taft, who eventually ran for mayor of Cleveland. Seth and his wife, Frannie, were baby-sitting me while my mother and uncle were away from home. Out on the tennis court, Seth held onto the fender behind me, keeping me upright while I pedaled forward. I still clearly remember the remarkable moment when I heard his voice, far behind me, saying, "Okay, you're on your own," and I realized I had mastered the wheel.

During his stay at our house Seth also read *The Wizard of Oz* aloud to me, introducing me to another way to travel. That was the first novel in my life, and it remained my favorite for years. I learned to read with that book: my mother would read aloud to me, and then when she quit, I would read on. "Okay, you're on your own." Over the next three or four years I read dozens of Oz books. Whenever I was lonely or depressed, I retreated to the Land of Oz.

Riding a bicycle and reading are called the two skills we never forget. I'm grateful for both, although I never went very far or very fast with the bicycle. Unlike my son Morgan, I never got "good" at it. I never owned a three-speed, let alone a ten-speed. The fanciest I ever got was to attach playing cards to the back wheel with a clothespin so my Schwinn would sound like a motorcycle, but I never had the desire to ride a real motorcycle.

Reading, on the other hand, had possibilities; I knew that early on. I asked my mother if there was anything I could "be" when I grew up, something that would put me to work reading books. She told me that the people who made books were called publishers, and that publishers had to read the stories first to decide which ones to make into books.

That moment, I expect, was the beginning of my life's journey into publishing, although at that time the prospect of becoming a publisher was no real contender for a boy who seriously expected to grow up and become a cowboy.

Just as I never got very fast on the bicycle, I never became a fast reader. There were theories about this when I was a schoolboy. Much later, my mother confessed to me that from the beginning she assumed I was probably not very bright, since I had been born so late in her life, and that she was surprised over and over each time those early tests revealed that I had a high I.Q. (No one ever told me how high, and I never asked. I suppose there's a statistic somewhere in some computer file that can be probed if they ever find out I'm the real Unabomber.) So why was I a slow reader? Because of bad teachers? Probably not; my peers passed me up. Teachers and counselors decided that I was just not "applying myself," that I needed more "effort."

Many years later my son Benjamin, who "tested genius," was helped in high school by special tutors and specially designed programs because he had what was by then called a "learning

Learning to Read and Write

disability," meaning, among other things, that he was a slow reader. (And a bad speller, which I also was. Horrible speller, well into my twenties.)

So perhaps I had a learning disability, and that's why I've always been a slow reader, and why I'm not a natural speller, and why now, as I type fast at the computer, I am forever trasnposing letters.

But I must confess that to a large extent my teachers were right: I wasn't applying myself. Because one of the things I learned early in my life was the easy path. I learned not to be suckered into needless effort and possible disappointment for the sake of competition. When I was in second grade, the teacher taught us how to count by twos and the difference between even and odd. She told us to get out paper and pencil and write down a column of even numbers, going as high as we could go, and to see how high we could go before the bell rang. Somewhere in the forties when I realized this was repetitive nonsense, I also realized I had an out: the teacher had said "could." I don't know whether I also realized that she had transformed a classroom of young minds into temporary robots so she wouldn't have to teach, thus setting an example of the easy path herself.

At any rate, I realized that excelling in math was optional. I put down my pencil and let my mind wander down the Yellow Brick Road to the Emerald City. When I was called back to account for the low score on my list of even numbers, I explained, "That's as high as I could go."

Ten years later I flunked calculus and failed to graduate from Andover with my class. Taking calculus had been optional, but once in it for a certain number of weeks, I had to pass the course to graduate, and I did not. To this day I don't know whether I couldn't or wouldn't pass that damned course. I believe I tried hard, and I know I suffered greatly from the failure. Truth is, if I could do it differently I would bail out sooner, not try harder.

I won't even get into the subject of sports, speaking of competition.

It was at Andover that I learned to love grammar, American literature, and writing. I learned how to bullshit there, too. The building for studying English was called Bullfinch Hall, which we shortened to Bull Hall.

Among my friends at Andover, one of the most significant was John Darnton, with whom I roomed for three years. By the time we became seniors we had grown apart. He was a disciple of Kerouac, and he spent his summer riding the rails; whereas my main influence was Doris Day movies, and my greatest goal was to sing in Andover's imitation of the Whiffenpoofs. But early in our friendship, when it was strong, we actually joked about literature and wrote fiction together, we quoted Holden Caulfield like scripture, and late at night we'd make up stories for each other, romantic yarns about imaginary girls we were going to screw, and how.

John went on to become a Pulitzer Prize winning journalist for the *New York Times*, and his first novel, *Neanderthal*, was a Random House best-seller in 1996.

As long as I'm name-dropping, I might mention a classmate named Jeff Putnam. At Andover there were lots of famous last names among the students, and you might guess that Jeff came from a famous publishing family. I don't think that was true, but he is now the editor for Baskerville Books, a distinguished small publisher of hardcover fiction in Dallas, Texas.

At Stanford I further explored the art of bullshit. As a slow reader in the English department, I really had no choice.

I became an English major pretty much automatically. Having no choice was a pattern for me, although I didn't recognize it at the time. After all, I was at college just because that's what a young person did after high school (or prep school). To the degree that I rebelled at all in that rebellious time of life, it was by choosing to go to Stanford instead of Yale. I chose Stanford because four winters in New England were enough for me, and because I too had read Kerouac and had decided there was something magical about California, although that probably had more to do with Doris Day.

I chose English because my brother Neil had chosen English nine years before me. Neil had also taught me to juggle and yodel and drive; it was natural that I should follow in his footsteps, even though he was an athlete and a fast reader.

American literature was a thrill to me, although I never made it through the complete reading list of any of my classes. That's where I learned to read enough, and just enough, to be able to write a good paper and write a good test. I got Cs, which by today's standards would probably translate to B+s. Whenever I'm asked if being an English major has any practical, career-related value, I have to answer yes. I can now digest a book-length manuscript in an hour or so and write an intelligent response. I may not read the work thoroughly or carefully, but I give it more focused attention than it would get from most other editors.

I also learned, at Stanford, when not to fake it. Once in a lecture course taught by Wallace Stegner, we were surprised by a test. I had read none of the works involved; I would "read" them eventually, but it was more efficient to "read" them after Stegner's lectures, not before. Caught unaware, I simply closed the blue book and walked away, leaving on the record that I had cut class that day. My girlfriend, Karen Mullenger, was furious with me; similarly unprepared, she soldiered on and did poorly on the test.

Karen and I sat side by side through many an English class, and she was a far better student than I. It infuriated her that I did not work hard. But why should I? I made a decision, halfway through college, that graduate school was beyond my ability and more important beyond my desire, and so a simple diploma was all I required from my four years at Stanford, as well as a good time.

As an English major, I was required to take some hard classes, of course, and I paced them as well as I could and squeaked by with my Cs, developing good reading lists and a library for the future. But my real education happened in the afternoons, when I took, over and over again, creative writing classes and life drawing. The life drawing has helped me some in my career; occasionally my cartooning skill has helped me design a book cover. The writing seminars (they weren't really classes) were very instructive. It was there, sitting around a large table, that I began to learn the skill of finding what was good in a bad story, and how to make a good story better. How to talk persuasively and publicly with an ego-driven author without offending. I learned a bit about writing, too, and got some of the worst stories ever written in English out of my system. I must thank Nancy Packer, who led at least half of those classes, for her sharp and entertaining insight. She eventually became the director of the Stanford Creative Writing Program, and I eventually became one of her publishers.

Another teacher to mention here is Yvor Winters. As an undergraduate English major, I was forced to take Winters's lecture course in American poetry, a course I detested as much as Winters did. I didn't really like poetry much to begin with, except for doggerel, for which I had (and have) a great talent. Winters liked only a handful of poets, none of them doggerelists. He was lofty and unsmiling, and he let us know he far preferred the company of Airedales to the company of undergraduates.

The reason I mention Winters here is that in time I became known as a publisher of Wintersian poetry. In time I came to agree with Winters that really good poetry is founded on rational thought and clear language, and those qualities need not be dull. I have also developed a taste for formal meter and rhyme (essential to doggerel), and I strongly believe that form strengthens, rather than constricts, a poem. I have published a few books of poetry in the "new formalist" school, which is identified by students and disciples of Yvor Winters. Among those poets I've published have been Charles Gullans, a protégé of Winters, and R. L. Barth, a close friend of Gullans and himself a publisher of Wintersian poetry. Being a publisher of new formalist poetry has given me a good excuse for not accepting manuscripts outside that school; unfortunately, I've also had to reject many manuscripts from within that school without having an easy way to do so; every poet, from every school, is eager to be published.

The most important author I've published from that band of poets is Janet Lewis, the wife of Yvor Winters. I first learned of Janet from Karen, who read her novel *The Wife of Martin Guerre* in a Stanford class taught by Charles Gullans. I liked her novels, which I read for pleasure, and in time I published her book *The Ancient Ones,* but that's getting ahead of the story.

My last quarter at Stanford I changed my minor. Having been hit hard in the soul by a comparative religion class, I had declared my minor to be religious studies, but I'd found out that religious studies had more to do with studies than with religion, and furthermore the religion involved was predominantly Christianity, in which I had little interest beyond how it related to choral music. There I was, slaving through two hard classes, hoping to get Cs and not too sure of it, when I realized that I had plenty of credits accumulated in the art department just by having spent half my afternoons for the past two years drawing naked people.

Just in time I quit my religion classes, once again thanking the insight I'd learned in second grade, this time bailing out in time.

ONE FOR THE BOOKS

By the time I graduated from Stanford with a degree in English, I'd also had four summer vacations, and in terms of training for the publishing business I had learned as much from my summer jobs as I had from my academic career.

The summer of 1961 I worked as a clerk in the House of Books, a small suburban bookshop in Dallas. I sold a lot of Nancy Drews and greeting cards, but I also learned about current bestsellers, and how exciting they could be. That was the summer of *The Carpetbaggers*. That was the summer of *Franny and Zooey*. Different as those two books are, I loved them both, and I think of them together because I was one of the first people in Dallas to read them. I also learned from the owners of the store, gruff curmudgeon Carl Gibke and his charming wife, Betty, how to treat a customer (and how not to), and that has made me, over the years, one of the best bookstore clerks in the business.

In the summer of 1962 I worked for the Red Barn Bookshop in a run-down neighborhood near downtown Dallas. The Red Barn was really an old red house, and the books were all used or antiquarian. The place was managed by Dick Bosse, a young bohemian who has since become one of the great antiquarian book dealers in the field of Texana. That was a relaxed summer, because Dick didn't care much for work and he very much enjoyed talk. I read a number of novels on the job, which, given my slow reading speed and Dick's chatter, was quite an accomplishment. It was there that I developed a strong taste for Richard Bissell, who remains my favorite American humorist.

Two incidents from my summer in the Red Barn stand out as important in my development. The first happened on the day Dick came back from appraising someone's atticful of books. He had a couple of cartons in the trunk of his car and we brought them in and unpacked them. There were a lot of hardback Zane Greys, which we priced at a dime apiece (I think they were first editions and are now quite valuable, but they were junk at the time). But the treasure, which Dick had picked up for a song, was a collection of Robert Frost poems, with a complete poem handwritten by the author on the flyleaf.

Another book Dick got his hands on from a catalog was a *Book of Common Prayer* inscribed by Caroline of Brunswick, Princess of Wales, to her ward, William Austin, in 1802. Dick sent me to the Dallas Public Library to find out who these people were, and I unearthed a story of royal scandal and international high jinks that obsessed me for years. I have written and rewritten and rewritten a novel about those people, I've collected books on the subject, and I've traveled to Kensington Palace and the Villa d'Este on Lake Como in search of their ghosts. I've never come close to making the novel any good, but the brief essay I wrote on the subject, which we displayed alongside the prayerbook under glass in the Red Barn, was my first piece of professional writing, the ancestor of the press releases and catalog copy I write regularly today.

The summer of 1963 was my first summer away from home. My Uncle Neil had arranged for me to be hired as a copy boy for the *Los Angeles Times* (Uncle Neil was a friend of publisher Norman Chandler), so there I was in the city room, getting coffee for reporters, sorting proofs hot off the Linotypes, tearing yellow paper off the AP and UPI wire machines, carrying books for reviewer Robert Kirsch, changing ribbons on huge noisy typewriters, learning about the power of ink.

I had an apartment on Normandie, in a polyracial neighborhood with palm trees, taverns, and delicatessens. I planned to use the summer wisely: to learn to cook, to write. I was twenty-one and I had a car and I was in a big, warm city; I also had college friends in town. I could have been social, could even have dated. But I missed Karen, who was up at Stanford learning about Janet Lewis from Charles Gullans, and my private life in

Los Angeles was dull to the point of being wasted: instead of cooking and writing and dating, I ate alone in a neighborhood restaurant each night and then spent the evening reading the works of Ian Fleming.

But the daytime excitement made up for my boring evenings. I put together weather reports that actually appeared in print. I ripped stories off the newswires and knew I was the first person in southern California to know what was happening in Selma, Alabama. That was the summer Kennedy went to Berlin and Jackie lost her baby. The Profumo affair broke, and *Cleopatra* opened, and I went to a special preview, as a member of the press.

I was supposed to have graduated from Stanford in June 1964, but I had been delayed by mononucleosis along the way, and so, newly married, I had one more quarter to go and one more summer vacation as well. I spent that summer at the Radcliffe Publishing Procedures Course in Cambridge, Massachusetts. I lump this summer with the others when I think of summer jobs, even though the "job" was academic, with classrooms and homework, and it cost, rather than earned, money. But the Radcliffe course didn't feel academic at all. The work and learning were practical, they made sense, they were fun, and I did it all joyfully.

The course, founded and directed by Mrs. Diggory Venn of lofty Boston society, was one of the first of its kind. Now there are dozens, but Radcliffe is still considered the best. It took young people, most of them young women, straight out of college and taught them all about a real working industry and then offered them the contacts and techniques to get them placed in entry-level positions. I felt honored to be accepted, although there were so few men there that I expect I got in without much trouble.

Learning to Read and Write

The first half of the course was about book publishing, and the second half about magazine publishing. It was clear to me from the start that magazines were fine but my real interest was in books. After all, I seldom read magazines, and I had always been a loving, if poky, reader of books. So although I worked hard during the second half of the course as well, what I remember, and what I'll describe here, was the first half.

Every day there were lectures and workshops, and then every evening there was about four hours' worth of homework. The subjects covered included every part of book publishing, from acquisitions to editing to design to typesetting to proofreading to production to promotion and publicity to marketing and sales to distribution. We had guest speakers every day, specialists in their fields, and they included authors and editors and booksellers and marketers and printers and on and on. Some of the speakers were stars of the industry: Austin Olney of Houghton Mifflin, Mark Jaffe of Bantam.

More than anything, I'm grateful to the Radcliffe Publishing Procedures Course for teaching me a vocabulary that I still use every day. I learned about picas, pubdates, signatures, serifs, cast-offs, and Girl Fridays. I learned the anatomy of the book: the spine, the deckle, the trim size, the type block; I learned why the copyright page is always on the verso of the title page, and I learned what a verso is, and why it's always an even-numbered page.

One speaker toward the end of the book part of the course brought in a stack of data processing cards and waved them at us. "You should learn something about data processing," he said. "It's going to become very important in the publishing industry one day." I thought that was vaguely interesting, but not relevant to me. I was no math major, after all, and my sour experience with calculus was only four years old. No, I was in it for the words, not the numbers.

And at the end of the course, I was ready to be placed, and Mrs. Venn was sure I was going to have a wonderful future in publishing. I did have one more quarter left at Stanford, but after that she would help me find a good entry-level position in the most exciting business in the world.

That prospect gave me a certain amount of security, but not a great deal of joy. The most common entry-level position for a young man who wanted to end up in the editorial offices was as a traveling salesman in the South. There were three key words in that phrase that I didn't like. And if I were able, somehow, with Mrs. Venn's help, to bypass the South and go straight to editorial, it would very likely be in New York, a prospect equally chilling.

As it turned out, I didn't have to cash in on my entrée. After coasting to graduation, I worked the Christmas season in a Palo Alto bookstore, then spent the winter reading *The Alexandria Quartet,* writing, painting, and working at odd jobs: as an aide in a nursery school, washing dishes, sketching a nude model in a nightclub act. Then in March Karen and I took off for an open-ended trip to Europe, a nine-pound typewriter hanging off my arm.

That trip did not have much to do with my publishing career except to postpone it at the start and to put it on ice at the end. While we were in London we were momentarily tempted by an offer from the Australian government to transport us down under for free if we would agree to work there for two years. We checked out the possibilities in publishing there, but before we got too serious we decided that move was too radical for us. I also considered taking a job as a scab bookstore clerk for Foyle's Bookshop on Charing Cross Road, but we rejected that one too and got on with our travels.

In Greece we found the island of Skiathos and settled there

Learning to Read and Write

for the summer, in a little house on a gentle bay a mile from the village. I returned to Athens briefly and bought supplies, including typing paper and twenty dollars' worth of paperback books, which back in 1965 was enough to last us the summer.

There on Skiathos I wrote my first novel, a dreadfully stitched-together collection of dreadful stories about a young man growing up to the wise age of twenty-three. Inspired by Lawrence Durrell, who wrote *The Alexandria Quartet* so fast and so on-a-Greek-Isle, I wrote like lightning.

Thoreau said books should be read as they were written: slowly and carefully. I'd always believed that, and not just because I'm a slow reader. I should also have listened to the converse. I thought my novel was wonderful, of course. I took pictures of it being weighted down by my pipe. I envisioned Tab Hunter in the title role. Because I believe in being kind to myself, I never reread that old material, but I am embarrassed about having shown it to anyone, and I'm grateful it never (of course it never) got published.

Nevertheless, that novel, *Oil All Over Your Address,* was a turning point for me because I did discover the joy of writing and the joy of accomplishment, and I decided to admit that I'd far rather be a writer than a publisher. Karen supported my choice; she had no great desire to live in New York, or the American South either. We decided to return to Palo Alto where we would both get jobs. I would work in a bookstore and write.

While we were in Paris (where I walked in the footsteps of Hemingway, read Updike, and wrote a short story) I wrote of this decision to my Uncle Neil, who had financed my upbringing and my education and who was, till his death almost twenty years later, the career mentor I repeatedly disappointed. Uncle Neil wrote back and urged me to reconsider: as long as I was going to work and write, why not work in the publishing industry and write? I wrote back and explained that I needed to put the writing first and that I wouldn't be much of a publisher if I were giving it my second best. I said I was glad I had publishing to come home to if the writing didn't pay off. Uncle Neil bought that, probably wise enough to see from my letters that I'd get hungry and insecure before I got to be a writing star.

So we returned to Palo Alto, where I walked right into a job as a clerk in the paperback division of the general books department of the Stanford Bookstore.

I very much enjoyed that job, and I was very good at it. The store, or at least that department, forcefully led by (Mrs.) Ted Davidson (also known as General Books), was a model of organization. The paperback division, happily led by Dick Henry, was equally well organized and full of jokes. This job put to use my skills as a host, a researcher, an arranger of books, a manipulator of index cards. I liked punching the time clock, I liked having co-workers, I liked bag lunches, I liked seeing new books arrive.

It turns out, I was working in a branch of the publishing industry in spite of myself, and giving it my all during my working hours. The only difference was that I was being paid peanuts, and I was working equally hard on my writing during my time off. I didn't mind that.

From Ted Davidson and Dick Henry I learned about sales reps and selling seasons and merchandising and cover design and returns and shoplifters and the difference between mass market and trade paperbacks.

Meanwhile, back in our cheap Palo Alto apartment, I was writing a blank verse novel about a mad bomber, sex, politics, poetry, and religion. Looking back on those young innocent days, I know now that I then knew very little about any of those things, but I was having fun. I also know now that writing is another extension of the publishing business; in fact, book writing and bookselling are the bookends of the business. But although I was a fine bookstore clerk, I was not yet a writer except in the sense that I wrote. I wasn't writing anything worth publishing.

One day, one of my former writing teachers, Blair Fuller, came into the Stanford Bookstore, and finding me there, he asked what I was up to. I told him I had completed a novel, and he invited me to show it to him. He was the West Coast scout for a new imprint, Paris Review Editions, which Doubleday was distributing for Blair's friend George Plimpton.

So I delivered *Oil All Over Your Address* to Blair Fuller, and sometime later (after Christmas, kindly) he called me and rejected it. I soldiered on with my blank verse novel, now called *The Fall of the Tower*, and when that was finished I foolishly sent that to him.

Wonders never cease. He liked it. He dropped by the Stanford Bookstore and told me so, and told me he was going to send the manuscript on to Plimpton. That news put me very high on my list of favorite writers. In time, or even in short order, Plimpton returned the manuscript to Blair, with a complimentary note. But the high feeling remained, and I now had the self-confidence to start what I expected to be my masterpiece, the novel about Caroline of Brunswick and her ward, William Austin.

But there is more to life than literature, and Karen got pregnant. When the time came for her to quit her job, we decided we couldn't make it on one bookstore clerk's salary, and so I started looking for other work. Naturally I explored the local publishing scene.

William Lane, the president of *Sunset* magazine (which also published books), had spoken to the Radcliffe course when I was there, and he had all but invited me to be his personal assistant/

valet, a lead I hadn't pursued at that time. Now it sounded like a good shot, so I put in an application at *Sunset* but was told there were no openings at that time. (I later found out that Mr. Lane went through personal assistants like candy. He was a demanding person, and the job was not easy or well-paid.)

There was a position open as a college traveler in the Los Angeles territory for the textbook division of Scribner. That was attractive: it may have been in sales, but college travelers were scouts as well. And although it meant being on the road, the road was all within metropolitan Los Angeles, a city I still loved, and I'd be home each night for dinner. Most of all, I liked the idea of working for Scribner, the former home of Wolfe, Hemingway, and Fitzgerald, not to mention the editor who had shepherded them all to fame. But I didn't apply for the job because Karen's two older sisters both lived in Los Angeles, and we didn't want to be that close to family.

I took an editorial test for the Stanford University Press. They sat me in a room with a dictionary, pencils, and an essay about one of the architects of the Russian Revolution, complete with notes and bibliography. My job was to clean it up. It was horribly punctuated, horribly spelled, and horribly written at every level, and I chewed it up with great pleasure. I spent over three hours on the test, enjoying every minute of it, and turned it in. When I got the results of the test I was informed that I knew my grammar and I was a fine writer and I was a terrible speller. Nevertheless, my writing skill was enough to make me trainable and hirable, and they would put me on a list of applicants eligible for the position of assistant editor, but there were no jobs open at that time.

The Stanford placement office got me an interview with Addison-Wesley, which had a division in Palo Alto for textbook publishing. The man hiring, the advertising manager, struck me as a nervous, unhappy, competitive nut, an unfulfilled

Learning to Read and Write

workaholic; and the routine he described, of slaving late into the nights and through the weekends, developing advertising campaigns for high school textbooks, sounded dreadful. I remained polite through the interview, which was late in the afternoon, and then drove home shaking with fear over what was to become of me if this was what real life and job responsibility were all about.

Fortunately, the problem solved itself, at least temporarily. The Stanford Bookstore offered me a promotion and a raise. I became the assistant manager of the textbook department, literally upstairs. The function of the job was to make sure books were available for classes. That meant getting the professors to get their requisitions in on time, making judgments of how large the class was likely to be, ordering the books, receiving and shelving them, then returning the remaining stock to the publisher after the class was over or transferring the books to another shelf for another class. It meant keeping lots of records and juggling lots of numbers. It meant managing a crew of low-paid flunkies who actually moved the books around. It meant badgering professors who didn't like to worry about practical details. It meant dealing with screaming, spoiled students when they didn't get their books in time.

I enjoyed the job for a while. I enjoyed the routine, including the coffee and the jokes with the people in my department. The most valuable thing I learned from the job was how to get on the phone and ask questions and make demands, even long distance. Call up Van Nostrand in New York, collect, and demand that they air-freight those damn books, the course starts Monday. That was a tall order for me, who was (still am) phobic about the telephone. But I learned to treat it as part of the job, and actually got a feeling of power when I was able to get something done that way, although I never got too good at it.

In time, I'm afraid, the position of assistant manager of the textbook department lost any charm it may have had for me. It was numbers, not words, and it was hard work all day long, and the only relief from repetitive routine was an occasional stressful crisis. I was smart enough for the job, but I was losing interest fast.

I still needed to make a living, though. We were a family of three now. I figured it was only a matter of time before I became a successful novelist, but in the meantime, I had to make a living. Against the greatest of odds, I applied for a Wallace Stegner Fellowship in creative writing at Stanford. I did not know how great the odds were against me, but I didn't expect to win the fellowship. No harm in trying, though, just like the lottery these days. After all, if I did win, that would guarantee my success as a writer, and my financial future. So I wrote up a proposal based on my plans for my historical novel, now called *Willikins Rex*.

Then I heard from the Stanford University Press. There was an opening for an assistant editor now, and they asked me to come in to meet with Jess Bell, the chief editor. Jess was a tall, self-confident Ivy Leaguer who was able to combine smart-ass and no-nonsense in the same tone of voice. He told me all about the Press: that they specialized in political science, especially Asian studies, that they manufactured the books right there, that they were dedicated to perfect English and strong writing, and that they were offering me four hundred and fifty dollars a month. That didn't sound like much money, even in 1967, but it was more than I had ever made before. The job sounded inviting: the chance to work with words until the words were right, and the chance to work for a small enough house that I'd see every bit of the process, from acquisitions through production to sales.

I told Jess that I was interested in the job, but there was still an outside chance that I might win a Stegner Fellowship, and I wouldn't know for another few weeks. Jess asked if I knew anybody in the creative writing department, and I said I knew Nancy Packer. He suggested that I call Nancy up and ask her if I'd been cut from the list yet. "She runs that department," he told me. "Those guys can't go to the bathroom without asking her permission."

I called Mrs. Packer and, somewhat embarrassed, explained my position. She said the committee had found my material interesting, but there wasn't much there to judge. Did I have any more I could send in? I told her about *The Fall of the Tower,* which Blair Fuller had liked, and she suggested that I drop it by.

Which I did. And a couple of weeks later the phone rang at dinner time and a woman's voice asked, "Is this the John Daniel who works for the Stanford Bookstore?" I admitted that it was. "Well then, this is Nancy Packer, and I have the great pleasure of informing you that you've been chosen to be one of our fellows next year."

The Wallace Stegner Fellowship in Creative Writing was one of the highest honors an unknown young writer could receive. It included a cash award of $3500, and my only obligation was to participate in an afternoon seminar twice a week. The seminar was a critique group of other fine young writers, guided by Stegner himself, or by a colleague of Stegner's. The best thing about the program was its prestige, which paid off not only in ego gratification but also in opportunities. Literary scouts were well aware of the program, and a Stegner fellow could be sure his or her book proposal would be carefully read by the best editors in New York. The names of now famous former Stegner fellows are legion. The year I was there, people were still talking about recent fellows Robert Stone, Larry McMurtry, Wendell Berry, James D. Houston, Shirley Ann Grau, Merrill Joan Gerber, Al Young, Thomas McGuane, and on and on.

My year, 1967-68, did not produce stars of that caliber.

Blanche Boyd has published a few feminist/lesbian novels, Peter Najarian has published a couple of small literary memoirs with Pantheon and North Point, William Hjortsberg has published quite a few novels but never became a household word, and Dean Latimer wrote for girlie magazines and eventually became the Almighty Editor for *High Times*. Among the other writers in the seminar (which involved the fellows, but also all the graduate students in the master's program in creative writing), I know of only a few who have made a career of writing. Henry Bean published an award-winning novel with Simon & Schuster and wrote the screenplay for *Internal Affairs*. Dale Peterson collaborated with Jane Goodall on a book about chimpanzees and went on to become a highly respected science writer. Mary Jane Moffat has become a teacher and anthology editor in the field of memoir and autobiography. I expect there are others, but I don't know who they might be. Anyway, our group did not produce stars, especially me.

    I don't think it was just a lack of talent that kept our class from making the big time. I think to some extent we were abandoned by the powers that be. For one thing, Wally Stegner had not been involved in selecting us; he'd been off in Vermont writing *Angle of Repose*. He was disappointed to find there were no "western writers" among us. That was also a year of tremendous unrest on college campuses, and Wally was dismayed by the lack of courtesy in the student community. That lack of courtesy extended to our gang, I'm afraid. People did not sit in awe at the master's feet, they sympathized with window-smashers, they dressed like pigs and overused words like *fuck*, and they were more interested in drugs and politics than in good writing. Stegner, of course, was a committed environmentalist, a liberal opposed to the Vietnam War, and a compassionate, truly good man. But he had no use for the decline in manners, and so he had as little as possible to do with us. There were no "western writers" among us anyway; that might have made a difference.

I don't blame Wally Stegner, or the turbulent times, for my failure to be discovered, however. The truth is I wasted that year trying to write *Willikins Rex,* that historical monster for which I was unequipped. I was invited by a couple of editors to submit manuscripts, and I did in fact send *The Fall of the Tower* out. William Decker of Dial gave me a blistering, thoughtful rejection in which he preached that fiction is about people, not ideas, a maxim I've kept and treasured ever since. Peter Davison of Atlantic Monthly Press wrote back that I was "crawling with talent" and offered me a $200 option on my next novel, which amounted to paying me not to publish *The Fall of the Tower.* Mark Saxton, who had just left Viking, was starting a new imprint called Gambit, to be distributed by Houghton Mifflin, and he took an interest in my writing, but I never produced anything he could publish.

As the year progressed toward spring, and I was involved in the process of choosing the next year's fellows, I was beginning to know (helped by the blunt appraisal of Peter Najarian) that I was clever but not great, and that this year was not going to be my stepping-stone to a writing career.

In spite of those regrets, I do feel enormously grateful for what I got out of the program. I learned a lot more from the seminars about appreciating good writing, and how to make good writing even better. That skill has helped me as an editor and as a teacher. I also made valuable contacts that have helped me in my later career. Herb Gold, who led the seminar the first quarter, provided a blurb for my novel *Play Melancholy Baby,* published twenty years later. I myself published two people from that class: Mary Jane Moffat and Constance Crawford. And I've published Nancy Packer twice. Moreover, I've traded on the prestige of the program often; I've dropped the words "Stegner Fellowship" shamelessly whenever I've thought it might help me get a contract or a publication or a teaching gig. Finally, I want to say that Wally Stegner himself was always a gracious friend to our press. He gave me blurbs for a couple of books, and I always felt that I could call on him for a kind of support that couldn't be measured commercially.

In June of 1968, knowing I was not on the path to greatness, I contacted the Stanford Press and agreed to go to work for them at the end of the summer. Then I took off to be by myself in Morro Bay for a few weeks. I wanted to finish *Willikins Rex* and be done with it. I did finish the second third of the novel, but then I quit and came back to Palo Alto. I put *Willikins Rex* in a drawer where it belonged and took a part-time job for July, baby-sitting the Jones Room in the Stanford Library where the Creative Writing Program held their seminars. I don't remember whether or not I was paid for that gig, but I do remember sitting at a big typewriter banging out sad, clever stories about a young man whose marriage and artistic career were both in big trouble. As a writer I was finally finding a voice, and it was sophisticated and blue. I continued writing these stories of suburban angst for another year or so, while I was working for the Stanford Press, and eventually stitched them into a novel I called *Addison*.

My job at the Stanford University Press lasted a year and a half. I signed on for two years, but when I left in the spring of 1970 I think Jess Bell felt the separation was best for all concerned. During my short stay I edited only three books. One was an account of a media feud in Meiji Japan by Kenneth Pyle, one was an assessment of Castro's performance in Cuba by Richard Fagen, and one was a study of political interest groups in modern Brazil by Phillipe C. Schmitter. I have nothing personal against any of those scholars, but their books meant nothing to me, and I also know they were destined to end up in a few libraries and the Stanford Bookstore and nowhere else. I must say, though, looking back, that editing academic prose for the Stanford University Press was the ideal job for the quintessential slow reader. When I was in a good mood, which I seldom was at that time in my life, I could treat the chore of untangling academic prose as a puzzle. More often I thought of it as a Herculean chore for which I had neither the muscles nor the motivation.

But let me also say that what I learned from the Stanford University Press, and especially from my boss and trainer Jess Bell, was substantial and invaluable. Jess taught me to edit. I already knew grammar, and I already could write, but Jess gave me a deeper understanding of grammar than I'd ever known, and his training showed me why I was a good writer and how to become better. I learned basic rules that have helped me to analyze my own writing and the writing of my students and authors, rules like:

Verb constructions are better than noun constructions.

The active voice is stronger than the passive voice.

Short Anglo-Saxon words are better than long Latinate words.

I also learned how to edit in such a way as to change the order of an author's words without hurting his feelings too much. An editor is not a butcher, but a helper. On the other hand, an editor must have the confidence to know he's the authority on language. The editor must also accept that the author is the authority on substance.

Another thing I learned, finally, in my late twenties, was how to spell. Not that I learned any magic rules for spelling in our labyrinthian language. I just learned that I could and should use the dictionary whenever there was the slightest doubt about the spelling of a word. I quit trying to bullshit myself and the rest of the world about this: you can't convince anyone that a misspelled word is better misspelled. Sometimes I didn't realize I didn't know a word; sometimes I still don't. But the greater percentage of my spelling mistakes came from my trying to fake it, and the Stanford Press and Jess Bell beat that out of me.

So I spent a lot of time at the dictionary, and while I was at it, I started reading Fowler's *Modern English Usage* for fun. Yes, fun is how I'd put it now.

I would edit about ten pages a day. Jess would go over those pages and write numbers in the margins and hand them back to me with a long typewritten critique in which he tore me to shreds by the numbers. Every now and then he'd draw a little pig-face in the margin. Occasionally, rarely, Jess would throw me a bone and say I'd done a nice job with a sentence.

Anyone who worked for the Stanford Press during the 1960s knows what an intolerant perfectionist Jess Bell was when it came to making books out of manuscripts. He drove editors to tears. He was also witty, outrageous at parties, and forceful in any conversation. The other driving force of the Stanford University Press was Leon Seltzer, the director. Leon was gentle and quiet, clearly brilliant and self-confident. People throughout the publishing industry had huge respect and affection for Leon Seltzer, who was one of the architects of the modern copyright laws. I hardly ever saw Leon, but I always felt both awe and comfort in his presence. Leon and Jess had nothing to do with each other socially. They were a working team.

One day while I was working at my desk I received a phone call from the publisher of a popular history magazine called *American West*. He told me that he was looking for an editor, and that Wally Stegner had recommended that he call me. This was like one of those gifts from nowhere, and I was delighted to join the man for lunch to discuss the possibility. I knew the magazine slightly; it was slick and full of pictures. Although history wasn't my bailiwick exactly, I liked the looks of *American*

West, and I knew for sure that it was read by a lot more people than any of the books published by the Stanford University Press. Things were looking up.

The lunch, however, was a failure. The publisher's agenda shifted as we got to know each other, and before the first course he was lambasting the current student community in general, my recent classmates in particular, and myself by implication for their/our/my disrespect for Wally Stegner, academia, and American society. He was right, I knew, but I also saw in him a curmudgeon I would be unable to get along with. Before dessert we were arguing about the Vietnam War, and by the time we left the restaurant we were barely cordial. I thanked the publisher of *American West* for lunch, we said a frosty goodbye, and I went back to the salt mines of the Stanford Press where at least the fellowship was comfortable.

As I've hinted, the late sixties were not happy for me. My marriage was effectively over, and Karen and our two young children had moved to Detroit. I was living in rented rooms here and there around the Midpeninsula, and my social life was nowhere. I was writing, but it was for my own therapy more than art. (I used up my remaining contacts in the publishing world by trying to interest them in my sad, self-centered novel, *Addison*.) The Stanford Press was scary and hard; I started each day by eating donuts and drinking coffee and reading the paper, trying to drag that out as long as possible.

When I got the word that my mother was seriously ill and depressed in Minneapolis, I took a leave of absence from the Stanford Press and went back to pay her an extended visit. Within a few weeks I turned that leave of absence into a permanent resignation.

I've written about my visit to Minneapolis elsewhere, and it doesn't have anything much to do with my training as a publisher, so I won't say much about it here. Only to say that I was once again off the career path. In fact I had no path. When my mother died in the spring of 1970 I was at loose ends, with no parents, no plans, no money, and no job. My only home was another rented room back in Palo Alto.

But I was in a better mood. As I drove across the Great Plains in June, I realized I was utterly free. I realized this was a wonderful time in history to be young and single and free. And, as a matter of fact, stoned, which I was at the moment. And which I stayed for quite a long time.

CHAPTER TWO

Deadlines and No Dead Lines

I SPENT THE REST of 1970 doing odd jobs for my landlord, drawing nudes and modeling naked, and partying more than I'd ever partied as a college student. I suppose I was grieving recent losses by overdosing myself with hilarity. I suppose I was finding myself and figuring things out. I smoked a great deal of dope and drank a great deal of cheap red wine. I was anything but a publisher, I wasn't writing much, and I don't remember a single book I read during that year. By the end of the year, I was ready for a bit of stability, which came in the form of a steady, if part-time, job at Kepler's Bookstore in Menlo Park just up the street from Palo Alto.

I also found stability in a relationship and a home that lasted for nearly ten years. The relationship was with Autumn Stanley, a brilliant and lovely woman I had met at the Stanford University Press. She was an editor there when I met her. She later became a developmental editor at Wadsworth Publishing in Belmont, and then left Wadsworth to be a freelance editor and scholar. We lived together in her home in Los Trancos Woods from 1971 to 1980. We were married in 1973, separated in 1982, and divorced in 1984.

ONE FOR THE BOOKS

I look back on the early seventies as my "clown days." I worked at the bookstore only three days a week, I took long walks in the woods, I got around town by the grace of my thumb, I acted in community theater, I joined the Palo Alto Models' Guild and displayed my naked body for art classes all over the Peninsula, I danced and partied with my bookstore friends, I meditated, I read the classics and pontificated on religion, I cartooned and did linocuts, clay sculpture, and other zany art projects in the basement, I smoked tobacco in handsome briar pipes and marijuana however it came to me, as often as it came to me. My hair was long, my shirts qualified as dresses, and I carried a purse; in those days such style did not mean I was a cross-dresser, just a freak.

Okay, that confession is over. My brother Neil recently referred to the early 1970s as my days as a philosopher. That was kind of him. I was a clown, taking being unserious very seriously.

My writing during the early seventies consisted of little humorous and philosophical surreal stories and sketches. Some of them actually got published in little magazines around town, but I was no writer then.

The most important thing I was during that period, for the sake of this focused memoir, and for the sake of my future, was a bookseller. The time I spent working for Kepler's Books was an important seven years, during which I learned more about the publishing industry than I'd ever known before. I learned about product and sales and trends. I also relearned the joy of working with that gentle segment of the public known as readers.

Kepler's Books was an important store, an intellectual focal point of the San Francisco Peninsula. It was known for Roy Kepler's brave pacifist philosophy and it was also the hippest place in town to be. Just being a clerk there gave me a minor status in my community; it also gave me a community of friends like none I've ever had before or since.

I started out at Kepler's as the returns clerk, sorting out a mountain of returns that hadn't been dealt with for months. I learned quickly that I loved shipping and receiving, I loved cardboard boxes and sealing tape and paper stuffing. I loved organizing stuff. I was a great returns department, a man of systems and lists. It was my first introduction to the whole concept of returns, a concept that has been a recurring (returning) theme, not always as pleasant as it was when I first met it.

From being the returns clerk, I took on more and more hours clerking on the floor of the two stores (Kepler's had a smaller branch in Los Altos), until I eventually had three full days of work. I enjoyed the work days as much as my days off, considering both equal in fun. I felt like a gardener in the bookstores, weeding the shelves, arranging the stock, making the order more orderly, watching the crop grow, get plucked, be replanted.

Some of my fellow clerks read on the job, but I did not. I did take books home from the store, books I borrowed and sometimes returned. I had anything I wanted to read at my disposal, and I took great advantage of that, but I never read on the job, because the job was alive and more fun than reading.

Anyone who has been a bookstore clerk knows the electric thrill of the Christmas rush, which starts right after Thanksgiving and builds and builds and builds until six P.M. Christmas Eve. The customers are happy, the books fly out of the store in bright colors, and the cash register goes jingle jingle jingle. I've always been sentimental about Christmas, and I love happy people, and I love books, and I love the party atmosphere, and it's also a time when a clerk can be the greatest help to a person in need. I've enjoyed every Christmas season I've spent in a bookstore, and there have been many.

ONE FOR THE BOOKS

In 1974 I took the Kepler's experience to a higher level. The buyer, Nick Simon, retired, and I asked Roy Kepler if I could replace him. Roy agreed, and I became a full-time, responsible employee with a decent salary and a challenging job. I started out with great vigor and lots of ideas, some of which I'd picked up while working at the Stanford Bookstore. I enjoyed reorganizing the store's inventory control systems, and we had a great team of young, energetic clerks making that store hum. Roy had recently doubled the size of the store, so part of my buying job involved filling vast space with stock, and in those days the paperback book business was growing madly. It was a buyer's dream.

I had a card file on every publisher, I kept track of the salesmen's visits, and I read catalogs. I also had the reordering system well organized, a legacy from Nick's days. And I improved the system for keeping track of current sellers, making sure they were ordered regularly from local suppliers and well displayed. I improved our regular shopping habits from the local distributors of mass-market and trade paperbacks and hardbacks, each of which came from a different source. It was a job of list-sifting, a task I loved.

I think I did well. That year's Christmas was the biggest in the history of the store, partly because we were a bigger store than ever before, partly because book prices had recently gone sky-high (though not as high as they were to become), but also because I kept the store stocked, using the local distributors daily and keeping track of everything that sold.

But, alas, I was not ready for full-time work, nor was I ready for that kind of responsibility. I freaked out. I couldn't handle it. The pressure of spending that much money was great. I wasn't ready to be a grown-up, and in the summer of 1975 I called Roy and begged him to let me off. Let me return to being a clerk, the happiest job I'd ever had.

Roy gave me my wish again, and I turned the job over to

Craig McCroskey, who had worked as the bookkeeper when I first started and had then gone to Oregon to be a librarian. Craig came back to Kepler's, became the buyer for a year, and then moved on to become one of the best-loved sales reps in the publishing industry. I returned to being a clerk, part-time, a job I kept until 1977.

I sometimes regret that I did not grow into the job of being the buyer at Kepler's. That was the obvious career move for me, if only I'd wanted a career. I might still be in that glorious business. Kepler's is now a powerful, modern store, and were I the buyer there I'd be at the top of my field. On the other hand, Kepler's is now battling Borders, and I'm sure the buyer has a full share of ulcers. Back then other possibilities were open to me as well: colleagues from Kepler's went on to start other bookstores—Printers Inc., A Clean Well-Lighted Place for Books—that have done well, and they invited me to join them. But I didn't. I wasn't ready.

Whether or not it was a mistake to step down from the position of buyer, I can say it changed me. I returned to being a clerk, but being a clerk was no longer as fascinating or as glorious as it had been. And so I eventually, gradually, cut back on the clerking part of my life and returned to being an editor. At that time relations between Roy Kepler and his staff were becoming acrimonious, and I found myself on the side of the staff. The whole thing was getting sticky, and I was itchy to get out on my own.

I started working as a freelance editor out of my home, which was actually the house of my wife, Autumn. The house was comfortably rustic, in the hills, on the edge of a pleasant wood, and I found the urge to work faint indeed. But it was a cheap way to get started.

Autumn was by this time a star editor for Wadsworth Publishing Company, which published textbooks for the junior college level, and her connections got me several assignments doing editorial analyses of manuscripts that editors were trying to acquire. An editorial analysis involves reading the manuscript and evaluating its strengths and weaknesses in terms of structure and style. A good editorial analysis praises the manuscript enough to please the author, so the author will sign a contract with the publisher and the acquiring editor will get the credit. This benefits the writer of the report, who will, of course, get more such jobs from the acquiring editor. A good editorial analysis also is a helpful tool for the developmental editor planning revisions down the line. The ideal editorial analysis results in the analyzer's getting the assignment of editing the manuscript. I became proficient at editorial analyses, and I churned out a lot of them. It's a skill I use today, sometimes to win publishing contracts, and sometimes just for a little moonlight freelancing to earn an occasional five hundred dollars.

The Wadsworth connection brought me several strange, rewarding jobs, during which I learned a fair amount about a number of subjects. I spent a few weeks in the Menlo Park Library checking facts on a sloppily written mass media textbook and found out a lot about the history of modern American popular culture. I wrote a chapter on the history of public relations. I wrote a sequence of short stories for a textbook on data processing. What I learned from that assignment is all out of date now, and it amuses me to think I banged it out on a manual typewriter. I also wrote an author's manual for Benjamin Cummings, another educational publisher. And I ghostwrote a book about a couple of modern Mormon families traveling about the American West making a documentary film about Indians. I got that job through a Wadsworth colleague of Autumn's, and it proved to be an important step, even if nothing ever came of the book itself. I learned that I could write credible, entertaining fiction for pay. (The book was supposedly nonfiction, a rewritten travel journal, but my job was to spice it up with plot and character, dialogue and humor, setting and style, so I call that fiction.)

The most interesting freelance job I got during the 1970s was as the editor/collaborator on a book about father-daughter incest. The author was Henry Giaretto, a therapist who had developed a treatment program for incestuous families in San Jose. The program was under the aegis of the criminal justice system, and it was a pioneer in its field. Incest was only barely becoming exposed, and Giaretto was a brilliant man with a lot of brave ideas. He was also a brilliant family therapist. But writing was not his forte, so I was hired to write the thing from scratch. I learned a great deal about incest in human culture, in mythology, in literature, in law, in pornography etc., and especially in American family life, where it exists a lot more than most people were willing to admit at that time. To my knowledge, the book never got published, although Hank had some good offers. By the time he got around to publishing, I think some of his ideas had become general knowledge and others had been generally rejected, the child sexual abuse field having been adopted by feminists and exploited by the mass media.

One great benefit of working on this project was that it got me out of the house. I did the work in an office at Hank's home high in the mountains, with a view of the bay far below me. Usually Hank wasn't around; it was just me and the dogs. In time I got bored with beautiful scenery and found the loneliness oppressive, and so I moved back down the hill. But I did not move my business back into Autumn's house.

Instead, I rented a tiny office in downtown Palo Alto. It was a brave and important move. I now had my name on a door. I now had my own telephone. Daily mail. Restaurants to eat lunch in. I was officially in business. I loved that little office, which I even used as a crash pad from time to time, stretching out on a floor space barely big enough for my body if I kept my arms at my sides. But the office was grand enough for me, my desk (a door on supports), my bookcases (boards on cinder blocks), my typewriter, and my ego.

In that office I edited a novel about Japanese prison camps in the Philippines and a book about stepfathers. That stepfather project was one I'm somewhat ashamed of. The man had a perfectly okay manuscript, an oral project in which he'd transcribed the stories of perhaps twenty different stepfathers. He wanted me to make a real book out of it. I couldn't think of anything to do but cut all the different interviews up and reassemble the material by subject matter: discipline, jealousy, money, rewards, etc. It was an interesting puzzle, and the author was pleased, and I earned a thousand dollars, but I don't think the book was any better after I was done than before.

I found out that the main thing my clients wanted from me was to come out of the relationship with a publishable book manuscript. That I could provide, but I couldn't guarantee that it would get published. I was scrupulous about warning clients of the odds against them. But authors are good at fooling themselves, and we'd go forward.

At first I took all the work I could get my hands on, so insecure was I. In time, I got to the point that I could pick and choose among my clients, and I could schedule them at my convenience, and they would wait in line. Nevertheless, I never got so self-confident that I could charge as much as I wanted. I always underbid, and I always was optimistic about how quickly I could do the work, so that I ended up working overtime to meet deadlines.

If what I've just written makes me sound industrious and happy in my work in those days, I should correct that impression. I was still, at that time, largely lazy and off-center. My typical day started with hitchhiking down out of the woods to catch a 9:30 bus to downtown Palo Alto. From the bus station I'd walk along the railroad tracks, smoking a joint, then turn up Hamilton Avenue, stop to get a cup of coffee, and show up at the office around 10:15. I'd put in a little time working, but as soon as the mail came, I read it eagerly and then wrote letters until noon. I was carrying on some very entertaining correspondence in those days—an activity I've almost entirely quit, along with a number of other pleasant but time-gobbling addictions. Then I'd go out to lunch, which often involved a beer or two, and after lunch I often took a nap on my office floor. Since the last bus out of town was at 4:30, that didn't leave a lot of time for work, which was the least favorite of all the things I did all day. (My favorite activities didn't begin until after the sun went down. That's when I got out of the house and prowled the piano bars of El Camino, singing and drinking. But that's another story.)

Having mentioned my correspondence during the 1970s, I should say that I look back on that as a fertile literary pleasure and exercise. I exchanged letters at least once a week for several years with Ray Russell, a science fiction writer and former *Playboy* editor whom I met in person only once (long after we'd already become good friends through the mail). He was a real craftsman with words, and a kind mentor to me, encouraging me in my writing and commiserating with me over my failure to get published. We exchanged stories, jokes, and limericks, but most of all, we exchanged cleverly phrased friendly conversation, which I consider an art worth practicing.

The other focus of my correspondence was a loosely organized gang of fellow writers and cartoonists consisting of Toby Tompkins in New York, Channing Bates in Rome/Paris/Santa Barbara, my brother Neil in Fort Worth, and myself. We called ourselves the Mountain Gorilla (I forget why; it was some invention of Toby's). We'd send out our poems, drawings, and stories and know they'd be passed around for all of us to read and comment on. Toby was the brilliant center of this gang, and his packages were worth the price of admission.

The point of that aside, I suppose, is to show that my wasting time was not a complete waste of time. But there's no denying that the correspondence always took precedence over the work. Nevertheless, I got some things done. I had goals of earning fifty dollars a day and writing five pages a day, and I accomplished those unambitious goals. In addition, I also accomplished two other more significant goals during that phase of my life: I wrote my first real novel, and I became a publisher.

Play Melancholy Baby started as a brash attempt to write commercial fiction, something that would sell. I decided to write within the mystery genre, because that's the only genre I knew anything at all about, although for that matter I didn't (and don't) know all that much about the genre and hardly ever read mysteries. But I knew a few basics of the subgenre called "amateur sleuth." A likable, quirky loner gets pulled into a case almost against his will, a person nobody likes is killed, everyone has something to hide, people fall in love and have sex, and there are the usual ingredients of plot-driven fiction: desire, danger, choice, consequence, and change. There was one basic that I didn't agree with, namely that the person what done it could be any one of the suspects, including the gentlest and nicest of the bunch. I didn't believe that. The most likely to have committed murder, I feel, is the asshole in the crowd, and so it's not much of a secret that in my book the jerk/victim is offed by another jerk. The mystery is in how to be sure and how to prove it and how to make others believe it without getting oneself killed in the process.

I wrote fast and furious, following an ever-changing outline. As the novel went on I found it straying from the standard model of the mystery. The killing didn't happen until more than halfway through, for example, and I found that parts of an earlier novella kept coming into the plot. The hero's own voice took over, and I let it. This guy Casey, my hero, is a piano player and a singer, a horrible dresser, a nut about old songs—my kind of guy. As he took over I realized that I wasn't really writing formula fiction, but I was having a great time writing the first real novel in my career. Casey and I became partners, and we've been together off and on ever since.

With all that was going on in my life at that time—there seemed to be an ongoing atmosphere of stress—it's hard to imagine when I found time to write a novel. I was not especially disciplined about it; rather, the story seemed to take over scraps of time whenever it could. The project's greatest progress happened in February 1977, when I escaped the Bay Area and went to Santa Barbara for a month. I rented a room in a cheap old hotel, spent my days on the beach and my nights writing. During that month I wrote about half the novel and outlined the rest, came up with the title, and realized that I was doing something really good. I had, in the words of Lawrence Durrell (and others), "found my voice." That trip proved even more important to me eventually, because it was a month of healthy habits—good diet, long walks, sunshine and fresh air, no drugs or alcohol, plenty of solitude, and lots of writing—and even more because it introduced me to the city of Santa Barbara and planted in me the idea of returning one day.

Well, the novel got finished, at least in its first revised draft, and thanks to my friend Rob Swigart I found an agent who liked it and wanted to try to sell it to the major leagues. This was Ellen Levine, a young woman at the Curtis Brown Agency. Ellen was wonderfully supportive, and she tried very hard, but she struck out. She did not consider the book a mystery, but a mainstream, even literary novel. I don't know whether she was right about that; perhaps she would have had better luck peddling it to a cheap mystery mass paperback house. But probably not. I expect she knew what she was doing. *Play Melancholy Baby* went into the drawer with my other novels, and I got back to work, licking my wounds.

The other major accomplishment of the late 1970s was that I became a publisher. In 1975 I established a tiny press that I named No Dead Lines. The name was chosen to represent two philosophies: that the work I published would be alive and lively, but more important, that the company would remain a hobby and not give me stress. I started with a separate bank account of a couple of hundred dollars, an official fictitious business name, an ISBN prefix, a logo (a cartoon of a quite self-satisfied frog), and a self-inking stamp that became my first stationery. My plan was to publish small booklets, each with a production budget of under a hundred dollars.

My first project was not exactly a small booklet; or, better put, it included a small booklet but was much more. The booklet contained four long narrative doggerel poems by my father, Lewis M. Daniel. These I reprinted by fast-print offset from a slim volume of his poems that had been printed after his death. I did the booklet in a limited edition of 30, bound in a linoleum-cut cover that I printed on a press I'd fashioned out of an old duplicating machine. Then, to accompany the booklets, I did a series of six very large (about three feet by four feet) linoleum-cut cartoon illustrations, correspondingly numbered. The project took me months and made me high as could be. I kept one set, gave sets to my three siblings, and then sold the rest of them for twenty dollars apiece and thus raised the bankroll that financed No Dead Lines. I'm very proud of that little enterprise. And even prouder of the work. I recently saw my linoleum cartoons framed and hanging in my brother Neil's dining room in

Fort Worth, and they hold up well, even for stoned art from the seventies.

At that time I belonged to a writers' group that met once a month in various homes to drink wine and read and critique each other's poems and stories. It began with a half a dozen friends, the nucleus of whom were Susan MacDonald and Rob Swigart. We called ourselves the Famous Writers' School, which, of course, was ironic because none of us were famous. The group grew over the years until it got too large and exploded and died; but in the meantime there were good evenings of good writing and good laughter.

In 1974, before I established No Dead Lines, the Famous Writers decided to produce an anthology of our work. There were eleven contributors. Each person was given four pages to fill, and each person chipped in thirty-five dollars and received twenty books. I did not contribute pages to the book, but I contributed cartoons throughout, and I was the coordinator of the publication, so I got about fifty books to sell through Kepler's and elsewhere. We made up the imprint "Limp Velum Press"; I no longer remember what that was all about. The title of the collection was *Famous Writers Anthology*.

In fall 1975 we repeated the venture, this time with fifteen contributors. Once again I contributed illustration instead of writing, and this time the book was published by No Dead Lines. Making fun of the building exploitation of the Bicentennial, we called this volume *Famous Writers of 76*. Both of these anthologies were printed at a local quick-print shop and bound at a bindery in Redwood City. My connection to Kepler's facilitated happy publication parties and a few book sales.

In the back of *Famous Writers of 76* I printed an advertisement for other limited editions from No Dead Lines. One was an eighteenth-century erotic poem illustrated by me in an Aubrey Beardsley style. Another was an assemblage called the

Gorilla Salon, in which contributors were invited to give me anything they wanted on 8-1/2" x 11" paper; they had to give me three hundred copies, which I then collated and bound and redistributed to the contributors, saving a hundred copies to sell. I think I sold enough copies to pay for my expenses, which were minimal. Also listed were two small forthcoming volumes of poetry by Rob Swigart and Nils Peterson. These two poets paid the production costs and I made a few bucks on book sales. This was my first foray into the exciting world of subsidy publishing. In the process I learned about getting things typeset professionally and about buying paper and about dealing with printers. (Rob went on to become perhaps the most nearly famous of the Famous Writers. He had a few comic novels published by Houghton Mifflin and then a number of mysteries and SF books published by St. Martin's Press, Dutton, et al.)

About this time I was also helping Autumn edit a short-lived literary magazine called *Stonecloud.* That experience taught me to dislike editorial committees, but I did enjoy the production part of the project: Letraset, pasteup, etc. It also afforded me the chance to get a few cartoons, poems, and stories into print.

Another learning experience was a course I took in San Francisco from Clifford Burke, one of a fast-dwindling number of great letter-press printers. I learned to set type by hand. I learned to build up a platen. I learned about paper and ink. And most of all I learned that I did not have the patience for that kind of publishing. I didn't much care for printing of any kind, as a matter of fact, except for art projects. Even when I was offered an offset printing press for free by my friend Buff Bradley, I turned it down. It was publishing I was attracted to, not printing.

One day a carpenter who was doing some repairs for Autumn learned that I was a small-press publisher and revealed that he was a writer. How often that coincidence has come up

Deadlines and No Dead Lines

ever since I became a publisher—usually to a groaningly awkward, quick conclusion. But in this case it was a happy meeting, because he was looking for a way to get his second novel into print at his expense. His name was Paul Fourt, and his pseudonym was Joe Cottonwood; the name of his novel was *Famous Potatoes*. I read the manuscript and liked it. We worked together; I edited and designed the book, he commissioned illustrations, and he also brought in a husband and wife who were getting started in book packaging. I bought Dan Poynter's book on self-publishing so I could learn and perform all the necessary steps like getting the book listed in *Books in Print* and getting a Library of Congress number. We worked for months and sent the book off to press.

Then the book packagers took the bound page proofs to the American Booksellers' Association (ABA) convention (I forget where it was that year) and sold the book out from under No Dead Lines to Seymour Lawrence, who had an imprint under the Delta aegis. I was paid for my editing and design and proofreading time, so I was not out of pocket. And I also received a hundred copies of the No Dead Lines edition of *Famous Potatoes* when it arrived. It was officially dead in the water, but it had become listed in *Books in Print,* and so I received orders and I filled them, legally or not. The project also paid off in terms of future work: Paul Fourt hired me to edit his next two novels in manuscript. He has since gone on to a fairly steady career of writing young adult novels, I understand.

No Dead Lines dramatically changed direction and complexion one evening at a meeting of the Famous Writers. I was there with Venetia (Vee) Gleason, a graduate of the Stanford Creative Writing Program now working in Stanford's administration. I don't remember exactly how it came about, but Vee decided that night to invest five hundred or a thousand dollars (an astronomical sum, either way) in the company. Over the next few days she and I became publishing partners, informally as far as the law was concerned, but partners nonetheless.

Within very little time she had rented an office in my building, and we were making plans for the No Dead Lines Storybook series, a collection of half a dozen short stories published as individual booklets in editions of one hundred copies each. The stories were by Vee and myself, Autumn Stanley, Susan Eastwood (one of the Famous Writers), Helen Chetin (a friend of Vee's), and Toby Tompkins (founder of the Mountain Gorilla). Good stories, cheaply produced, well sold, broke even. Didn't satisfy Vee, I'm glad to say. We were soon on to bigger things.

One of the most important things Vee brought to No Dead Lines (besides good taste, humor, and friendship) was her close association with Janet Lewis, the poet/novelist I've already mentioned with admiration. I felt honored just to be introduced to this gracious, plainspoken, merry and wise woman who was in her mid-seventies. Imagine how thrilled I was when she agreed to have No Dead Lines publish her new book of poems, a short collection about her travels to the land of the Anasazi.

The Ancient Ones, as the book was titled, was a significant leap up for No Dead Lines. Gone was the hundred-dollar budget. We lined up Daniel Mendelowitz, a renowned artist and emeritus professor from Stanford, to provide lovely illustrations, and we produced an elegant, nearly square paperback volume with brown ink printed on textured brown paper. We did an edition of three hundred copies, which we sold for $7.50 each. We made a handsome brochure which we mailed out to Janet's and Daniel's mailing lists, and the edition sold out in about three weeks. We quickly went back to press for another four hundred copies, and they lasted another year or so.

Vee and I learned a lot about printing techniques from *The Ancient Ones*. But the two main lessons for me were the value of spending some money to get things done right (that was no problem for Vee, but it's been a problem for me all my life), and the pleasure of direct-mail marketing to a small fan club. That still remains my favorite way to sell books.

Janet's influence on No Dead Lines continued. Our next project was *Recall the Poppies,* a book of poems by Marjorie Bryant with illustrations by Della Taylor Hoss, both of whom were friends of Janet's. We made a very pretty little book, and we sold it out quickly through direct mail and at a publication party at the home of the local chapter of the Sierra Club.

The next No Dead Lines book was also by a friend of Janet's. This was Hildegarde Flanner, a marvelous writer who lived in Calistoga. She was the sister of Janet Flanner and had sold essays to *The New Yorker.* I had never heard of her, but Vee assured me (as I presume Janet had assured her) that Hildegarde was highly respected within a small circle of old-time literary appreciators and collectors. That's all it took. We made contact with Hildegarde and soon we were on the way to publishing her long environmental essay *A Vanishing Land.*

A Vanishing Land was an expensive book to produce. The typesetting cost more than we were used to (having typeset only poetry before), and this was also our longest book and our first perfect-bound book (since *Famous Writers of 76,* which hardly counted). We did an edition of five hundred copies of which we sold about three hundred. I don't think we broke even, but by then we could afford to take a small loss. The more important thing to say about *A Vanishing Land* is that it was a beautifully written book, an example of how magically good prose writing can be. I've never been much of a reader of nonfiction, but this essay was thrilling to read, and I'm still proud of having published it.

A Vanishing Land was the last book published by No Dead Lines.

Vee was getting busier and busier with painting and the piano, and I was getting busier and busier with my freelance business. The business now included not only editing and ghostwriting, but also book design and production and small-press consulting. I put together a multicultural resource handbook for a team of Stanford graduate students; I designed and produced a storybook for a fellow Kepler's bookseller; and I advised Meredith Phillips, an old friend, on how to market the first book published by her imprint Perseverance Press.

Having acquired a taste for publishing, I wanted to do it for profit—not by selling books, but by selling my services as a maker of books. I knew I couldn't do that with Vee because for her publishing was art and not business; so I established another imprint, which I called John Daniel, Publisher. Its purpose was to publish books for pay. I tried to avoid the label "vanity press" and instead coined the oxymoronic "private publishing." Vee and I still left the door open to publish occasional books together as No Dead Lines if we became so inspired, but it never happened.

The only book to be published under the John Daniel, Publisher imprint back in those days was *Mother to Myself,* a collection of posthumous poetry by Pami Djerassi, a young woman who had committed suicide. The book was financed by her mother, and it sold out quickly to friends of the family. I also put into production an advice book called *You and Your Money,* by Kathryn Hlebakos, a San Jose radio announcer that I had an aural crush on. But while that book was still in page proofs I sold the project to Celestial Arts, assuming that was a step up for the author (wider distribution) and a feather in my cap (a sale that made me an official book packager). Alas, Celestial Arts underwent changes shortly thereafter and the book was never published.

Memorial Day Weekend, 1979, I went to the American Booksell-

Deadlines and No Dead Lines

ers' Association convention in Los Angeles. I had been to an ABA before, when it was in San Francisco in 1976, but that time I'd gone as a day-tripper and a bookstore clerk. I had in fact also tried at the 1976 ABA to meet with Ian Ballantine to interest him in a book illustrated by Gerde Wegener for his Peacock Press, which would earn me a finder's fee and some valuable contacts, but Ballantine successfully eluded me. But primarily that 1976 ABA had been just a lark for grabbing free books and scoring some free hors d'oeuvres and cocktails. That's what most bookstore clerks did (still do?) at ABA.

In 1979, though, I went with a lot more professional purpose. I went as a publisher (my badge proved it). I went there to shmooze and reestablish contacts I'd made during my years at Kepler's. I wanted to see what other small-press publishers were doing—the publishers who were small, but large enough to be exhibiting. I also took with me a sheet listing the book projects I was working on: the stepfather book, a World War II memoir, the Mormon/Indian book, and the incest book. Playing the role of agent, I dropped this sheet off in publishers' booths, hoping to get some nibbles. I handed out my business card promiscuously, trying to score some editing or production work down the line.

As far as I know none of these efforts paid off, although I've come to believe that you can never really assess the value of attending ABA, since the long-term pay-off of shmoozing is one of the things that keeps publishing alive. But I never sold any of the projects I was agenting.

What did happen, of course, was that I reverted to my bookstore-clerk behavior and grabbed all the free books I could lug up and down the festive aisles, those free canvas shopping bags getting heavier and heavier, hour after hour, day after day. And night after night I raced from party to party, drinking and smoking and flirting and making an ass of myself like Pinocchio in funland.

About two weeks after I got back to work in Palo Alto, I woke up one morning with more pain than I'd ever experienced before (or have ever experienced since) completely occupying my right arm, from neck to fingertips. I felt immobilized by pain, but staying still hurt as much as moving. So I dragged myself to work, where I found that I could not hold a pen or pencil without excruciating, electric pain. Nor could I type. I was knocked out of work.

It took a long time to get better. I went to a chiropractor, then a neurologist, then a shiatzu massage therapist, then an acupuncturist, and finally a physical therapist. Eventually I did recover the use of my arm and fingers, although the last part of me to heal was the thumb and two fingers with which I hold a pen. For that matter, the tip of my index finger is still slightly numb, a lifelong reminder.

I was forced not to work for about three weeks, during which I stayed home and read. What did I read? All the freebie books I'd lugged around the floor of the ABA, which were, I'm sure, part of the reason I had this pinched nerve.

But the excesses of the ABA were not entirely responsible for my functional breakdown. I had long suffered from stiff necks and back problems, as well as from chronic upper respiratory problems and bouts of depression; and I had been warned by one wise healer, "John, you'd better change something about your life, or you're going to go on suffering from one physical ailment after another."

Bingo.

Recalling that the healthiest and happiest I'd been in years had been the February I spent in Santa Barbara, I decided to go away again when winter came. It didn't matter where I went, especially; I just wanted to get out of town by myself and write again. I wanted to haul out that nearly completed historical,

Willikins Rex, and finish it up to close that unsatisfied chapter of my life.

It took longer than I'd expected to get my affairs in order, but I finally did get out of town in March 1980. I went to Wilbur Hot Springs, a country spa that Autumn and I had visited as guests a number of times. This time I went on a "mellowship," Wilbur's cute name for an extended work exchange. I worked for the hotel four hours a day, for three months, for which I received meals and a bed in the dormitory.

In fact I received far more. I got my mental, spiritual, and physical health back as spring took over the countryside. I also finished the novel *Willikins Rex,* but that accomplishment was secondary by a long shot. The important part of those three months was chopping kindling, washing dishes, making beds, cooking, doing windows, meeting people, greeting people, milking goats, swabbing floors, clearing brush, taking walks, and soaking in hot mineral water.

It's curious that I would write about this experience when it was publishing that I was specifically *not* doing, but I think not being a publisher for that period of my life was an important part of my development as a publisher.

When I returned to Palo Alto I was unable to return enthusiastically to my office and my business. I had had a taste of country life, healthy habits, being outdoors, and being in a community. I wanted to keep all those things for a lot longer than a three-month vacation, and I wanted them as more than just a fond memory.

And so, when Richard Miller, the owner of Wilbur Hot Springs, told me his plans to bring in a new staff, and that he wanted me involved, I decided to move back to this place I loved so much. Autumn decided to come along. The business came along too, because I was still filling orders on the Djerassi book, but the business died off fairly quickly once the books were all sold. (For that matter the marriage was dying as well, and eventually Autumn moved back to the Bay Area.)

I stayed at Wilbur Hot Springs for two years. I was not a publisher. I was not a writer either, although I did write one long story, a historical piece about my Irish-American ancestors. My only attempt to get something published was to send *Willikins Rex* to Ellen Levine, the agent who had tried to peddle *Play Melancholy Baby*. Ellen did not like *Willikins,* and that was the end of that. I was bothered by her decision, but I knew she was right and that all the time I'd spent on that project was valuable only insofar as the writing itself had been good for me.

It didn't bother me that I was no longer a writer, because I was so happy being an innkeeper. Eventually I became the general manager of Wilbur Hot Springs. I worked my butt off, deliriously happy in my work. I enjoyed working!

I also learned how to play the guitar better, progressing from "Home on the Range" to "The Folks Who Live on the Hill," a quantum leap in sophistication. That's important too, even though it wasn't exactly publishing. It was an aspect of my innkeeping life that I kept into later chapters, and provided a continuity that helped me reenter the world of books gracefully when it was time to do so.

From being an innkeeper I learned how to say no, how to stick to and enforce rules, how to manage a staff, how to value thrift, how to spend some money, how to cater to people with oversized egos, how to judge for myself what was right for myself and when to sacrifice my own wishes and when to hold on to them. All of these lessons have helped me ever since. I also thank Wilbur for giving me a vacation from publishing when I needed it most.

I left Wilbur a stronger man, eager to try out my new strengths. I did not intend to reenter the book world. Instead, armed with a

Deadlines and No Dead Lines

guitar and a repertoire of a couple of hundred popular standards, I returned to Palo Alto, hoping to start a career as an entertainer, playing and singing in clubs and restaurants. I suppose I chose Palo Alto because I knew the territory, and because there were remnants of a marriage that had to be dealt with there. But also I knew I would need a day job until I found job security in night life, and I figured I could always pick up hours clerking in the bookstores I knew so well.

I experienced a couple of setbacks in that area. Kepler's wouldn't have me, because Roy had a policy against revolving-door quitters; he and I had not parted under the best of terms in any case. Printers Inc., the other big store, which was owned by several of my friends from Kepler's, wouldn't have me either; Susan MacDonald would not take on anyone who wasn't willing to commit to two years. But within a few days I did find a job in Kepler's of Los Altos, now separately owned by a former tavern owner named Tom Thorpe.

Kepler's of Los Altos was in sorry shape. Tom was struggling valiantly, but the store was a mess, owing to circumstances beyond his control. Since I'd worked in that store in the early 1970s, a Tower Books had opened in the shopping mall across El Camino. It was now the reign of Reagan, and the South Palo Alto/Los Altos/Mountain View community no longer remembered the social virtue of shopping at Kepler's, and this wasn't really Kepler's, anyway. The grand problem, though, was that the landlord of the shopping center had no sympathy for the store and obviously wanted Kepler's out of there so he could generate more income from the space. And the specific problem at hand was the parking lot, torn into a war zone so that no customer could park within easy walking distance of the store.

As a result of these problems, poor beleaguered Tom Thorpe was on hold with most of the major publishers, the store looked shabby, he could not afford or attract any help other than inexperienced kids who'd work for minimum wage. He hired me in mid-September as buyer and general manager, hoping I'd be able to hold the store together through the Christmas season.

I did that, organizing the buying habits so that we bought books, periodicals, and calendars weekly from Milligan News, Ingram, and Bookpeople, and bought from nobody else except for special orders, which we prepaid. We kept on top of things and we did get through the Christmas season with the cash register ringing enough to keep the store open, even if collection wolves were howling nearby.

But shortly after Christmas the coup de grace arrived in the form of Crown Books, which opened a store on El Camino, just outside our shopping center. The parking lot, eventually restored, became a parking lot for Crown instead. As our stock dwindled, so did our traffic. I tried putting out a newsletter to attract customers, but we couldn't give it away except to the few customers we already had, most of whom didn't care. I tried moving more and more of the stock into the front room, making the shelves there look full, and converted the back room into open space, which I hoped we could get the community to use for book discussion groups. But it was dingy and depressing, and the community ignored us. I brought my guitar in on Wednesday nights and tried to create a coffee-house atmosphere, but that seemed to discourage customers rather than attract them—which probably should have told me something about my plans to be a professional musician.

Speaking of which, that wasn't going so great either. Having started well, playing for fifty bucks a night in a restaurant four nights a week, I thought I would make it; but after that gig died I went from one-night stand to one-night stand, in coffee houses and restaurants and occasional wedding receptions. Eventually I found that the effort of chasing gigs exceeded the pleasure and certainly the financial reward, and by the time I gave up on Palo

Alto I was playing only once a week, for tips, at an ice cream parlor, competing with the happy bleeps of a Ms. PacMan machine.

The truth is, I was getting a lot of pleasure out of music. I loved practicing, I loved learning new songs, I loved singing in piano bars as a customer. But it was becoming clear that I was not going to survive financially on my musical talent. A similar thing was going on in my social life: I enjoyed living in apartments in Mountain View, and I was fond of my roommate, Irene, but I had no social (or sex) life, and knew I would not have a social (or sex) life until I resolved the issue of my dying marriage, which clearly had no future, at least no future that I wanted anything to do with.

Not a good time of my life. In June of 1983, I read an article in *Newsweek* about independent publishers, which profiled two small presses in Santa Barbara. They were Capra Press and Black Sparrow, both of which I'd admired as a bookseller. The article referred to the town as a mecca for small publishers. I already thought of Santa Barbara as a place of joy and health. It was again time for some change.

I put together an impressive résumé and wrote letters to John Martin and Noel Young, the owners of Black Sparrow and Capra, respectively, and told them I wanted to work for them and why they should hire me. Rather to my surprise, I got a note back from Noel Young saying he was thinking of taking on an intern, so when I got relocated in Santa Barbara I should give him a call. I rushed to the phone and called him right away.

It was lunchtime and the man who answered the phone at Capra was David, the part-time shipping clerk. Nobody else was in the office. Not knowing what the word "intern" meant, I asked David what job was available, and David told me it was the job of sales manager.

Hot damn, I thought. I called later in the day, spoke to Noel Young directly, told him I wanted that job, and asked him when I could meet him. He had no memory of my original letter or my résumé or his note, but he told me he would be in San Francisco the following week, and he agreed to meet with me there.

The day I met Noel Young in a bar in the Haight-Ashbury district of San Francisco, my back was in spasm. I know there was a meaning for that spasm, the first I'd had in a year, but I don't know what the meaning was. Was I frightened about another life change? Guilty for plotting to leave Palo Alto for good? Nervous about displaying my minimalist list of professional accomplishments at the age of forty-two?

I needn't have been nervous about meeting Noel. He walked into the bar smiling, we introduced ourselves, and he ordered the first three beers (one for me, two for him) in a series that was to get well into double digits before the afternoon was through. After preliminaries we proceeded to a Chinese restaurant for lunch and more beer and got down to business.

Noel explained that his sales manager, Stephen Williamson, was leaving Santa Barbara, going to New York to break into bigtime publishing. Noel was looking for a replacement, and he wanted to know what were my long-range goals in publishing. I said I'd eventually like to acquire and develop manuscripts.

"But that's what *I* do," Noel said. "Making the books and getting them into the warehouse is easy. The hard part is moving them *out* of the warehouse. Do you think you'd have a talent for that?"

"I don't know," I confessed. "I'd like to try." I told him I was coming to Santa Barbara whether he hired me or not, and that I'd do anything at all to get my foot into the door in the publishing community down there. This may not have been a smart thing to say in terms of power negotiating, but it was the truth, and while I'm not self-righteous enough to say the truth has always served me well, I can say that the truth is usually the easiest position to take, and I'm all for easy.

We agreed that since I was coming to Santa Barbara anyway, starting with two trips down in my station wagon hauling my stuff, I should stop in at Capra and we'd have more lunch and more beer and discuss the matter further. In the meantime he'd be interviewing other prospects, and I'd be checking out more possibilities. Then Noel invited me along to his next appointment, drinks with Randall Beek, who was then the main buyer for Bookpeople. That provided me with a chance to do a little more name-dropping before driving back down the Peninsula, my back already feeling much better, either from the beer I'd drunk or the die I'd cast.

I gave notice to Tom Thorpe, and on August first I was once again without a job. Within a few months, Kepler's of Los Altos went out of business, by which time I was working full time in the publishing business in Santa Barbara.

CHAPTER THREE
Two for the Books

MY MOVE TO Santa Barbara was made easy by my friend Channing Bates, my fellow Mountain Gorilla, whom I'd known since we were boys together at Andover. Channing's parents had moved into a retirement community, and he was house-sitting their former home until they could make arrangements to sell it. The house was a beautiful, sprawling place high in the hills overlooking Montecito and the Pacific. So I had a fine place to stay until I could get myself settled.

My first goal was to find a day job in publishing. I had a couple of meetings with Noel Young at Capra, where I also met Susan Winton, the woman who was obviously going to take Stephen Williamson's place as sales manager. I wasn't really disappointed that the position was already filled, because that's the part of publishing I felt least prepared for. But since Susan had worked for Capra for a couple of years already, her assuming the job left a vacuum, namely the sales manager's assistant.

Noel made no firm commitment and no generous offer, but he did say he could take me on at least for a while, at least part-time. In the meantime I was free to explore other options and see if I could find another job.

Two for the Books

As Noel knew, I'm sure, jobs in Santa Barbara's publishing community are rare. There was (and still is) a lot of small-press publishing going on in this town, but it was made up mainly of cottage industries, one-book publishers, and self-publishers who didn't want or couldn't afford to hire help. I did get sort of an offer from Patricia Bragg of Health Sciences Publications out in Goleta—Patricia wanted someone to manage her whole business—but I wasn't interested. So I signed on with Capra on a temporary, part-time basis.

Channing and I rented a house in town and moved out of that palace on the mountain. I went about the business of making Santa Barbara my home town: renting a post office box, getting a phone, finding a dentist, a barber, and a car repairman, making new friends, starting with Channing's cousins, attending the Unitarian Church, taking classes at Adult Education, and learning the piano bar scene. I got to know musicians in the local jazz scene in hopes of getting my music act together (literally). But the greatest part of my new home town was my new job, to which I walked happily in the mornings, stopping along the way to pick up a donut and coffee.

My title, as Susan's assistant, was Publicity, which meant writing press releases and catalog copy and designing ads. But the job also entailed busywork galore, such as typing invoices, filling out forms for the Library of Congress and *Books in Print*, wrapping packages, making deliveries, Xeroxing, filing, emptying trash, etc. It appears that I proved myself, because shortly after I came aboard informally I came aboard formally, working full-time and being paid with an actual paycheck.

I learned an enormous amount working for Noel Young. Noel was a former printer, and although printing technology had changed a lot since he'd set type, he still loved the production part of the business and was happy to throw all kinds of knowledge around the office, which I fielded as fast as I could:

trim sizes, paper weights and colors, print runs, cover coatings, half-tones, veloxes, pmts, etc. It was from Noel that I learned most of what I know about making books and getting them into the warehouse.

I also learned a great deal about the business side of the business, but that was mainly from working alongside Susan Winton, who was capable, kind, and conscientious. It was from Susan that I learned everything I know about moving books out of the warehouse: sales reps, advance sales, drop ships, purchase orders, special orders, prepaid orders, phone orders, charge cards, overdue accounts (whom Susan called "bad guys"), and on and on.

My first major assignment as Publicity was to arrange a party celebrating Capra's big book of the fall 1983 season, *The Couch Potato Handbook*. I got press releases placed with all the media, lined up a bar for the event, and arranged to have half a dozen televisions brought in from a thrift store. Having the Couch Potato authors in town also meant a party at Noel's house, where I got a chance to play the guitar and sing.

For a singing career was still on my agenda. At the start of my new life in Santa Barbara, with only a part-time job, I had both the time and the financial need to keep practicing, shmooze with musicians, hunt for work, and play in public whenever I got the chance. And indeed, after I played up at Noel's house for the Couch Potato party, Noel got me a paying gig at one of his local watering holes, the Metro. The gig did not last long, but it brought in some welcome spare cash.

Sometime early that fall I wrote a press release for a new Capra book, an anthology called *Women Writers of the West Coast*. It was a good release, I remember, and I was especially proud of having arranged the list of contributors in such a way as to form the profile of a breast, a gimmick that probably went entirely unnoticed by the world, but pleased me. What did get noticed, by Marilyn Yalom, the editor, if not by me, is that her name was spelled "Talom" in the bold headline. This mistake was discovered after the review copies went out. The typo, my first major typo in Santa Barbara, was discovered late Friday afternoon, just before the staff and the rest of Noel's gang were to quit for the week and wander over to the Metro to hear me sing.

I felt awful for the first time that fall. At one point during my first set I spoke into the microphone and said, "You know, this isn't my only job. I also have a day job of which I'm very fond. And it's for my fellow workers at Capra Press that I'd like to dedicate this next song." Whereupon I launched into "Call Me Irresponsible."

The people at Noel's table laughed, and I felt forgiven and almost weepy with relief. I hoped especially that Susan had forgiven me and wondered briefly why her approval mattered most to me.

Later in the fall Capra took a giant step and bought a computer and hired a programmer to develop a system for a small publishing company. The system, dubbed "The Little Giant," was to handle general ledger, accounts receivable, accounts payable, royalties, inventory control, etc., and of course the computer was also available for word processing and mail merge. It's hard to believe that as recently as 1983 Capra Press was, though hardly a pioneer, making a brave and costly investment to enter the computer age. Not many small publishers were there yet.

This was my first hands-on experience with a computer. The fact that I was doing simple, repetitive tasks (cutting invoices, mainly) did not matter; I felt all-powerful. I could also see that this was the beginning of a big change in the way America would do business, even at the small-press level. I used my publishing connection to help my friend Steve Rogers buy one of the first Macintosh personal computers. And my eyes widened further.

Another important event for me that first fall was that I got the chance to edit one of Capra's best-selling titles, *Great Hot Springs of the West*. As a former hot springs manager and a former ghostwriter, I was a natural for the job, and the job needed doing quickly. I did it, and then had the pleasure of pasting up the pages, which consisted of columns of type and photos. A year later I was to help develop the text for an even more successful book for Capra, a charming book of cat photographs called *Ernie*.

The most important thing to happen to me in the fall of 1983 came in December, when I fell in love with my supervisor. This may sound like personal rather than professional news, but this development, this new partnership, was and continues to be the most significant thing to happen to my entire publishing career. Not to mention my personal life. From this point on, I should stop writing in the first person singular, because nearly everything that's happened to me in publishing from December 1983 forward has happened to us, and every step I've made we've made together.

At this point, though, Susan and I were still working for Noel Young, still two employees of Capra Press, with no firm future plans. It is a risk to begin a relationship with a close fellow worker, to start spending nights with a person with whom you spend your days. But we took that risk and won. Capra won too, at least temporarily, because our partnership made us work all the more efficiently.

We did, however, have an alliance that went beyond our allegiance to Capra Press, and Noel jokingly said he could see the writing on the wall. He claimed credit for bringing us together, and now he could foresee the time when we would leave him and get out on our own.

But in the meantime, we were working together well for him, and our relationship as a couple was not based on future plans. We spent the winter and spring of 1984 in the bliss of a new love affair. Working together by day, frequenting the jazz joints and piano bars in the evenings, sleeping together by night. I still occasionally visited the house I rented with Channing, but my real home was in Susan's house, with Susan and her boys and her cat.

The ABA convention of 1984 was held in Washington, D.C. Noel and Susan went together, leaving me to run the Capra office by myself for a few days. I did a half-assed job of running the office, just processed some mail and answered the phone. I was doing some serious pouting, because I didn't get to go to the ABA. I was doing some even more serious fretting because Susan was off at that highly charged convention with a man whose devotion to the pursuit of parties was a Santa Barbara legend. So I stewed through the weekend. I tried to jog away my jealousy, and I threw out my back in the process; that was the last time I've ever jogged. I also got busy and contacted a couple of entertainment brokers in Santa Barbara, hoping to revive my music career, just in case my job at Capra and/or my relationship with Susan turned out to be in serious danger.

When Susan and Noel got back from Washington, the ABA party was still going on for them. Some new friends who had partied with them in Washington came up from Los Angeles and there was a big dinner at a Montecito restaurant, where I felt like a green observer, an invisible outsider, an unattractive wallflower. The party was to have continued, with a breakfast planned for the next morning, but I told Susan I wasn't interested. She was on her own for that one.

Whether or not I deserved Susan's kind attention at this point, she gave it to me. She made up an excuse to tell the Los Angeles contingent, and she and I spent the next day alone together. We went to a hot tub place and rented some privacy and talked seriously about where our relationship was going. That was the first time we ever discussed the possibility of our having a professional future together.

We began to plot our long-range escape from the frying pan of Capra Press into the exciting fire of our own small business.

My goal at that time was to become a successful "private publisher." I'd invented the term, but not the profession. It meant I would produce books for people, and perhaps eventually companies and institutions, for their own private use and private distribution. I figured Santa Barbara had a good population of potential customers, wealthy people who would hire me to publish their poetry collections, memoirs, family histories, philosophical essays, etc. I would edit, design, and produce their books, and I would deliver those books to them. They would pay me handsomely for the service. I would also give them some advice on how to get their books reviewed by their local paper and placed in their local bookstores, and how to send out an announcement to their friends and family, but it would be understood that the challenge of disposing of the books would be up to the author/customer.

I also wanted to publish a book now and then at my own expense, something I admired and felt I could sell enough copies of to break even. The marketing of those pet projects would be primarily by direct mail, as I had marketed the Janet Lewis and Hildegarde Flanner books I'd published from No Dead Lines.

Susan endorsed my dreams and joined me in planning what was to be our future. She had business skills to add to the mix, and enough sales experience to add to the scope of our marketing scheme. Why limit ourselves to direct-mail and home-town marketing? Even the privately published books deserved the benefit of our marketing skills—to the degree (sometimes not much of a degree) that such books could be marketed.

I had a bit of money left over from a small inheritance from my Uncle Neil. It was only about four thousand dollars, but it gave me the courage to drop my hours at Capra Press to half-time. (I had also signed on as a member of I. Newton Perry's society music organization, and was picking up some spare change playing for cocktail parties in Montecito. That gig didn't last very long, and while it lasted it didn't make me rich, but it helped me believe I could safely lower my income at Capra.) I rented a very small office in the Fithian Building, down the hall from Capra Press, and installed a carpet, a phone (with a listing in the Yellow Pages), a desk, and a Macintosh. I was in business. John Daniel, Publisher.

This name, John Daniel, Publisher, was the name I'd used for private publishing in Palo Alto. But this time Susan and I decided to use the name for our royalty imprint. For copublishing, we picked the name Fithian Press, after the building. The Fithian Building was at that time the unofficial "publishers' row" of Santa Barbara, and so the name "Fithian" had literary connotations for the home town. During the time we spent in that building, we saw many publishers come and go, including Capra Press, Ross-Erickson (gone by the time I got there), Jim Cook Editions, Joshua Odell Editions, Olympus Press, and our two imprints, not to mention many book designers, typesetters, graphics companies, a literary magazine, and a newspaper. Right next to our little office was the larger office of Jim Cook, a typesetter and book designer from whom I learned a great deal about typography and book production.

Next came the challenge of finding authors. Looking back, I find that last sentence hilarious. If there's one thing in the world of which there's no shortage, it's authors. I've found in recent times that the challenge is in avoiding authors without being obnoxious about it. They're everywhere.

Of course I was looking for two specific kinds of authors: for John Daniel, Publisher, I was looking for distinguished literary writers who would let us bring out their works in small, elegant editions for a fairly limited audience; for Fithian I was looking for any decent author who would pay us to publish.

For our royalty list of distinguished authors, I looked to the Bay Area, the place of my literary roots. Within the first year I had signed on books by Stella Zamvil, Janet Lewis, Hildegarde Flanner, Mary Jane Moffat, and Joe Cottonwood (aka Paul Fourt), all of whom were friends from former writing and publishing days up north. I should add that I did not expect to finance all of these publications; I accepted loans from the authors for some of them, but I won't say which. This is a practice I've continued—occasionally to accept loans from authors for non-subsidy books. These loans are paid back promptly in the form of separate large royalties. The purpose of this arrangement is to allow us to publish a book that we would not otherwise be able to afford. (I've often been asked by prospective paying authors to use the John Daniel imprint for their subsidy books—indeed, sometimes the royalty imprint is requested as a condition of the contract—and I reject all such offers.)

In the next couple of years, the list of books by Bay Area authors continued to grow. We added Nancy Packer, Joan Baez, Sr., Charlotte Painter, Constance Crawford, with second books by Moffat and Baez; second and third books by Lewis; and second, third, and fourth books by Flanner. In subsequent years we did a third by Baez, and we now have a second book by Packer. As years went by we added a few more Bay Area authors, including Maclin Bocock Guerard and Richard Fagen (both connected to Stanford), but we relied on that community less.

I don't have the time, nor would readers have the patience, for a boastful description of all these early books. I do want to

Two for the Books

say, though, that I'm very proud of having published three opera libretti by Janet Lewis, even if they did not sell well. I'm proud of having brought out the autobiographical writings of Mary Jane Moffat, who was (and is) famous for her course in how to write memoir. The socially significant memoirs of Joan Baez, Sr. are very meaningful to me, and they have sold quite well. And perhaps most important to me are the four books we published by Hildegarde Flanner, the last four books of her distinguished career. Hildegarde (who was not technically of the Bay Area, but from the Napa Valley to the north), had such magic with words that to read her prose is a transforming experience. As for working with Nancy Packer, that gave me not only a sense of pride but a sense of fulfillment, Nancy having been my favorite teacher at Stanford.

I also want to say that most of these early books by Bay Area authors were successful. They attracted impressive blurbs from famous names (Wallace Stegner, Kay Boyle, Evan S. Connell, and Al Young, to name only a few); they were well reviewed in *Publishers Weekly*, the *Los Angeles Times*, the *San Francisco Chronicle*, and elsewhere; the book signings were well attended and profitable; and the direct-mail campaigns paid off handsomely. I am enormously grateful to my Midpeninsula (and Napa Valley) authors for establishing John Daniel, Publisher as a legitimate, grown-up if small-press, publisher in the literary world.

Working with these Bay Area authors required a number of business trips back to that area. These trips were frantic and fully scheduled. Susan and I would drive into the Midpeninsula and stay with Meredith (Merry) Phillips, my old friend and now the proprietor of Perseverance Press. The trip usually involved a book signing at Kepler's or Printers Inc. for a new book, which in turn involved dinner with the author. During the day before, we drove around and visited all the authors we were courting or who had books in production. We always worked into each trip a visit with our friend Vee Gleason (my former partner in No Dead Lines), a visit with Janet Lewis (who continued to age but never got older), and, after the signing, a late evening at Mac's Tea Room, the piano bar that had kept my spirits alive during my last year of living in that area. (Alas, sometime in the late 1980s we went to Mac's and found that it had been turned into a disco. The last of the Peninsula piano bars, and the end of a musical era.) The evening would end even later, with a gossipy chat with Merry, our host, who never retired until the wee hours of the morning. We would return to Santa Barbara the next day, exhausted but feeling productive, often with a new contract in our briefcase.

Now would be the right time to mention that my mystery novel, *Play Melancholy Baby,* finally found a home in print. As I said above, Meredith Phillips had established Perseverance Press to publish mysteries, and she was off to a good start with two already in print. I sent her my book, and she wanted to publish it if I would agree to some revisions. Her editing greatly improved the book, and it was published in 1986 to good reviews and modest sales. I arranged for Perseverance Press books to be distributed to the trade by Capra Press, which was to the benefit of Noel Young, Meredith Phillips, and myself. The book signing at Kepler's in Menlo Park was a sentimental success for me, attended by dozens of old friends I hadn't seen for quite a while and haven't seen since.

I was now a small-press author as well as a small-press publisher, and I've traded on that dual identity ever since.

Attracting Fithian Press authors turned out to be a snap; acquiring them was hard work. Nowadays we get quite a few contracts from repeat authors and referrals, but back then we relied on a system that Susan and I invented and have been refining ever since. We got John Daniel and Company listed in *Writer's Market* and its sister volumes *Poet's Market* and *Novel and Short Story Writer's Market* and invited submissions. That's when I learned just how many writers there are in the world.

The brown envelopes would arrive at the post office and I'd shlep them to the office. I'd shovel through them and divide them into three piles: the gems worth considering for our royalty list (only a few each year, so this wasn't really a pile); the outright rejects, which were books that specifically oughtn't to be published because they were so poorly written, or for some other reason (too big, outside our area of interest, etc.) oughtn't to be published by us; and the rest. The rest we shlepped home, to be read on the weekend.

That's how Susan and I spent our weekends back in those early years. Both of us, in the back yard during the summer, by the fireside during the winter, reading through big piles of manuscripts. Our goal was to find something nice to say to each author, to find a reason to reject the manuscript that did not hurt the author's feelings, and to introduce Fithian Press and let the author know, in a non-pushy way, that we'd be happy to consider the book for a copublishing venture if the author ever decided to go that route.

I know this sounds sneaky and dishonorable, but I believe we were doing a good thing. We received many, many thank-you letters for our rejections, because we were the only publishers who had actually read the authors' manuscripts. Of course we did not read complete manuscripts, but we did pay attention to the author, and it was appreciated.

And it paid off. Authors would write back, thanking us for the rejection and asking for more information about Fithian Press. We'd supply the curious author with our brochure, accompanied by another personal letter, and he or she would send the entire manuscript back. I'd read it more carefully this time and, unless I found something amiss, offer the author a copublishing contract. By now there were usually friendly phone conversations as well. And in time we'd be in production, copublishing a book.

I think what made it work was our friendliness, our honesty, the quality of our production, and the earnestness of our marketing and distribution efforts. We also allowed the author unlimited free copies that he or she could sell, thus increasing the author's chance of recovering the cost of the project. When an author sold books, he or she kept all the money from those sales; when we sold books we paid a high royalty based on our net receipts.

I expect now is the time to come to the defense of subsidy publishing. We have had to endure occasional snide remarks in print, calling us a "vanity press," and there is no denying that Fithian authors do subsidize their books. The closed literary establishment has always officially frowned on this sort of arrangement, assuming that the only proper publisher is one who risks his own money. The idea being that the publisher must risk his own money in order to motivate his sales and marketing efforts. Another idea being that if the book isn't going to make it in the marketplace, it isn't worth publishing.

These ideas are not only wrong, they're self-righteous posturing. In these times, perhaps because of television and the pervasive dumbing down of our society, literature simply doesn't sell except at the superstar level. Any literary publisher who relied on book sales to stay in business would go broke fast or at best barely get by. Let's be honest. New Directions survived for decades because James Laughlin's father was rich. Several of the most distinguished and celebrated "not-for-profit" literary presses have full-time employees hired just to write grant proposals. University presses rely on the academic tit. Other houses

I know have other sources of income: rental income, a printing business, subsidiary rights sales, etc. I admit that occasionally a small, independent publisher will come up with a "best-seller" that makes money; then that money is part of what subsidizes the less successful books on the publisher's list. I also want to add, without naming names, that many, if not most, publishers large and small accept secret subsidies. They consider it none of anybody's business how the books are financed, and they're right. What the hell, I will name a name: Simon & Schuster published the history of my Uncle Neil's company, Dresser Industries. I don't know the details of that deal, but if that book was successful in terms of book sales, the sales involved only one large customer.

Yes, Fithian Press is a subsidy publisher. We avoid the term "vanity press" to distance us from the scoundrels who earned that name, companies like Vantage Press, whom I name only because they became the subject of a class-action suit; I understand they've cleaned up their act since then, but I still don't think much of their books or their distribution efforts. Vanity press scoundrels—and there have been many—promise the moon to their authors and deliver a few copies of a shoddy book. If the author wants any promotion or marketing, it will be up to the author. If the author wants more copies, the author will have to pay for them (after already paying for them to be produced). Vanity press authors are disappointed people.

Fithian Press has never operated that way, and our authors are our friends.

Another thing I could mention at this point is that some of the Fithian Press books, which are not narrowly defined by the niche of belles lettres, have far outsold our John Daniel and Company books. To be fair, I admit that some of the Fithian books have not sold well at all, but in those cases small sales were expected, and we made sure our authors knew about their slim chances before signing a contract. We feel a book is a success if it reaches its audience, even if the audience is only the author's own circle of friends and family. Toward that end, we do all it takes.

The financing of a small-press publishing company is, I expect, a laughable subject to anybody who really knows money. When I established No Dead Lines in the 1970s, I put in some money and Vee Gleason put in some money and I tried to spend nothing but money we already had, from those original endowments and from book sales. We kept things so small that that was possible, although Vee sometimes wanted more elegance than we could really afford. My rule was not to mix my personal wealth with business resources, lest I go broke.

As for John Daniel, Publisher/Fithian Press, it started with personal wealth, the aforementioned pittance of a legacy from Uncle Neil. Then Susan came into an inheritance when her stepmother died, which was some forty thousand dollars. That allowed her to quit her job at Capra and devote her time to our company instead. (I was still working at Capra half-time, and I took over Susan's post as sales manager.) And yes, we did use personal money, until it ran out, by which time our company was limping along, but still not strong. Then I came into some money, another forty thousand, thanks to the sale of some land in Mendocino. So I quit my job at Capra and we and the company lived on my cash infusion while the company got stronger and stronger. By the time all the money we had was gone, the company was up and running, and we were able to draw a salary.

My brief period as sales manager at Capra Press was instructive. It's not that I learned so much about the business operations; working alongside Susan had made me pretty knowledgeable, thanks to the osmosis of our relationship. But I did learn a bit about when to be tough, when compassionate, when to be realistic and when to dream. I was also happy to give the job over to Noel's wife, Judy, when the time came for me to leave.

In addition to the Bay Area, we began early to cultivate Santa Barbara for authors, for both of our imprints. We were already known in publishing circles, thanks to our association with Noel and Capra. I also got involved with the Santa Barbara Writers Consortium, which was a pleasant group of local writers who put on programs and readings. I joined their board of directors and published a cooperative anthology for them for a couple of years. Susan and I also organized a book fair as part of the annual Santa Barbara Arts Festival for a couple of years. I put in some time at the Writers' Lunch, which happened every other Wednesday in the restaurant downstairs from our office—a loose association of local writers, stars and wanna-bes alike, who hovered around Barnaby Conrad. I contributed some writing to *Santa Barbara Arts* magazine and to *Connexions*, a local literary magazine put out by our friend and colleague Jim Cook.

This hometown shmoozing paid off. In our first John Daniel catalog we were able to list a poetry collection by Perie Longo, who had (and has) a strong influence on the local poetry scene. We published a photo-essay book by Betty Williams about the development of her vineyard. And we presented a book about the Chumash Indians, published in cooperation with EZ Nature Books and the Santa Barbara Museum of Natural History. Other royalty local authors early in our history included Kit Tremaine, Gene Knudsen Hoffman, Jeff Greenwald, Leslie Cady, and Sean Hutchinson.

We found there to be a bit of a risk involved in publishing local authors on our royalty imprint, John Daniel, Publisher. Of course, that's the imprint everybody wanted, and this town is teeming with writers. We didn't want to accept just anybody, even if they offered us generous loans, and so we were bound to hurt some feelings. We also wanted local writers to value Fithian Press and copublishing, and not consider it second-class treatment. But we did have to take local authors on occasionally, if only to show our sincerity to the community. It's important for us to have something of value to our local bookstores and local newspapers, too. In more recent years we've been able to present some pretty important books in terms of the local literary scene: nonfiction by Cork Millner, fiction by Dennis Lynds, anthologies edited by Steven Gilbar and Sheila Golburgh Johnson. These books may not have had big sales nationally, but they've clearly established us as one of the most important literary publishers in town.

Meanwhile, we did in fact find some local authors happy to copublish under our Fithian imprint. We did quite a few small books of poetry for local poets, all of whom know each other. We also did a number of memoirs by residents of the Casa Dorinda, a retirement community in Montecito. Our reputation spread by word of mouth, and the reputation must have been a good one, because people were knocking on our door.

I have my favorites among the local authors who have copublished with us, and it might get me into trouble to mention some and not mention others. But I do want to voice my affection for Lee Foster, an elderly resident of the Samarkand retirement home. Lee walked into our office one day with a bundle of papers and asked how much it would cost to turn them into a book. I thought I was dealing with a nut here, and I wasn't sure I wanted to take on what looked like an impossible puzzle of a production job. It was his life story, mixed in with his philosophy of choosing a retirement home for himself and his invalid wife. I looked it over and estimated high: seven thousand dollars. Lee pulled out his wallet and took out a folded piece of paper, which became, unfolded, a blank check. He filled out the check for seven thousand dollars and grinned, and we shook hands.

Two for the Books

We ended up publishing five books with Lee Foster, all about aging. He was one of the most cheerful people I've ever met, even as he celebrated aging and death. He couldn't write for sour apples, and he knew it, but writing—four hours a day—was a therapy more valuable for him than medicine or psychiatry. We did our best to make his books readable and handsome and available to his own audience. He had dozens of friends, and therefore sold dozens of books, and he had no wish for any greater success. We enjoyed his business and his company, and when he died we were sorry to say goodbye.

Another favorite local author has been Phil Albaum, who was not our author exactly, but a self-publishing author for whom we did editorial and production and marketing as freelance consultants. Phil's book was about his experience in World War II and, by extension, his wife Judy's experience as a survivor of the Holocaust. As it happened, when Phil first came to our office Susan was out at the airport, sending her older son off to college for the first time. She came back to the office in tears (joyful tears), and Phil said she was acting like a Jewish mother, which Susan admitted proudly she was. We became fast friends immediately and have remained so.

Our association with Phil Albaum was also the beginning of a trend for us to publish a lot of World War II memoirs and books on Judaica and the Holocaust. Phil's fascination with both subjects has led him to establish the Res Gestae Foundation, for which we are official advisors and board members. And we've copublished so many books in these two areas under our Fithian Press imprint that we've put out little specialty catalogs in addition to our annual general catalog.

Back on the national scene, I knew we were getting somewhere when Leonore Fleisher of *Publishers Weekly* named us second runner-up in her joke contest for "smallest publisher in the land." (Meredith Phillips's Perseverance Press was first runner up.) This was an early milestone, not only because it got us ink in our industry journal (big deal), but because it gave us a chance to state our mission: to succeed in small small-press publishing. A challenge verging on oxymoron.

Which leads inevitably to the subject of growth. Throughout the history of our business we've dealt with an approach-avoidance conflict around the subject of growth.

One way to measure our growth has been in terms of office space. The office I first rented when I dropped to half-time at Capra was little more than a closet. Susan and I could barely fit in there together. We then moved down the hall of the Fithian Building to a room with no windows, about the size of a small bedroom. But it was big enough for two desks and another table for the computer. We kept the closet-sized original office for a shipping room. Next came a larger office, back down the hall, next to the closet, which we gave up. This larger office had two windows, and enough space for some bookshelves and a wrapping table. Then we teamed up with Jim Cook and wheeled our stuff once more back down the halls to a huge suite with all sorts of windows. Jim took half the suite for his typesetting business (and his bed), and we took the other half, with enough room for three desks and a computer station. I never much liked that office, although it had space and a false fireplace. The State Street windows admitted city dirt, and our suite-mate, much as we loved him, loved grand opera and cigarettes. In 1990, which is where this memoir will officially stop, we left the Fithian Building, which by that time was threatened with earthquake renovation and would emerge from that battle too expensive for artists and publishers.

I just mentioned that our last office in the Fithian Building had three desks. By that time we were relying heavily on the talents of Eric Larson, who did all kinds of editorial and production chores for us. He was also picking up knowledge of typesetting and book design from Jim. At that point he wasn't on our payroll (even Susan wasn't on our payroll, for that matter; she just worked more than full-time), but he was becoming an important part of what we were doing. We also relied on help from interns and volunteers—my sons, Morgan and Ben; Susan's mother, Barbara; and a UCSB student named Mandy Syers—who came in on various schedules throughout those years in the late 1980s. So we easily filled whatever space we had, and when the time came for us to leave the Fithian Building, we had outgrown even the half-suite.

Another index of our growth was the expansion of our storage capacity. We started with one stack of books (a thousand copies of *In the Time of the Russias*) in the corner of the closet-sized office. That became two stacks, then four, and by the time we moved out of that office we'd become overwhelmed and had rented a storage "unit" at a local self-service storage company called Budget U-Stor. It didn't take long to outgrow one unit, then two, then four, then two much bigger units, and eventually we took over a big caged area of an old former avocado processing plant out behind Budget U-Stor. That became two cages, then three.

One thing a small press can count on is inventory. It's much easier to get books into the warehouse than to move them out. This is especially true in the subsidy press business, which was accounting for more and more of our operations. I understand that some subsidy houses, including Northwest Publishing Company, print only a few hundred copies of a title, with the promise to go back to press "if necessary," knowing full well that "necessary" will seldom happen. That's probably a good idea, but not our policy.

Yet another index of our growth has been the tracks of our baby steps into the modern world of technology.

I have this vision of two boxes. One is labeled "What in the world would I want this stuff for?" and the other is marked "How in the world did I ever get along without this?" In box number one, at the time of this writing, are e-mail, the Internet, caller ID, and a bunch of other gadgets that I haven't heard of and don't want to learn about. In box number two, the essentials, are the computer, the fax machine, the copier, Mr. Coffee, the answering machine, the fancy telephone with multiple lines, the push-button phone for that matter, and Susan's accounting software, to name a few. The entertaining truth is that most of the items in box number two used to live in box number one. The television, however, is still in box number one, although the compact disk player just made the leap.

I am a Luddite. I am a sympathizer with, if not a member of, Bill Henderson's Lead Pencil Club. I long for the days when to do business across country meant getting on a train and riding for days. I think one of the reasons I'm in the literature business is that I like small, I like slow, and I am nostalgic rather than futuristic. If I could leave this business it would be for something that does not require always learning new tricks.

But, whether I like it or not, the publishing business, even at this level, requires learning new tricks all the time. New technology for book production. For sales and marketing, distribution and fulfillment, accounting. I don't think of this as a particularly competitive business (another reason I'm here), but I wouldn't dare give up the computer on principle, because we'd be left in the dust.

So our technology has grown. A baby Macintosh to begin with, then a Mac Plus then a LaserWriter then a hard disk then several Macs with fancy, space-age names, our personal copier along the way turning into an office copier, a shared fax machine becoming our own fax machine, the rotary dial phone becoming the push-button phone which eventually got attached to an answering machine and then took on call waiting which was replaced by a phone "system" costing thousands of dollars offering a bunch of features that nobody in our company understands. We now take MasterCard and Visa and we have a toll-free number. We have Acumen, a software system designed for small publishers, which takes care of accounting and inventory and a whole bunch more. We even have an e-mail address, which Susan checks in on about once a week, but that's getting ahead of the scope of this memoir. The point is, we've grown, and you can probably tell I'm not one hundred percent in step with it emotionally.

The biggest challenge for any growing small press is distribution. If you're doing only a thousand copies of a book, and only an occasional book, and you're putting them out mainly for private or personal dissemination, then you don't need distribution; but if you're building a list, and if you do a few thousand copies of each title, and if you're committed to getting those books out to the world, and specifically to the trade, then you need to have a distribution plan. I was fine without distribution when I published as No Dead Lines; nor did Susan and I need distribution to sell our first few books by direct mail and place them in Kepler's Books. But as we began to build a list with some potential, including the first Moffat book and the first Baez book, it was clear we needed to have some way of getting our product out there in the marketplace.

We began by having our books placed at Bookpeople in Berkeley, which took only a phone call to our old friend Randy Beek. Bookpeople did not actively sell to the stores, but they served as a wholesaler from whom stores could order. We also made a similar arrangement with Inland Book Company in New Haven, Connecticut, so the books would be available on the East Coast as well.

I've always celebrated being small, but growth is a sexy seductress. Susan and I went to the ABA convention in San Francisco in 1986 as members of the Capra Press team, but since Noel needed only one of us, we took turns having time off. I used my time tearing up and down the aisles of the Moscone Convention Center, renewing contact with every friend I'd ever had in the book business. I made hundreds of notes on my memo pad, passed out hundreds of new business cards, shook and reshook hundreds of hands and grinned hundreds of grins. I was manic, frantic, on fire. I was announcing to the publishing world: I'm ba-a-a-a-a-ack! Having worked for Capra Press for two and a half years, and now having established a company of my own, I wanted people to recognize me, which they did. I wanted more people to recognize me, which they did not. I began to learn something about ABA conventions from the point of view of the publisher: they're an emotional roller-coaster ride. You look at the publishers who are bigger and more successful than you, and you get horribly depressed, feel like a worm. Then someone shakes your hand and you make a note on a memo pad, a note that may turn into a sale down the line, and you think that might help your growth, and you find yourself sailing, you're Mr. Big. This manic-depressive curve is a rapid, bouncy ride, the cycles happening several times a day, sometimes several times an hour. In the meantime you're working very, very hard, all day long, and in the evening you're partying very, very hard, which means in effect that you're working very, very hard. All in pursuit of growth. I love it. I hate it.

The next year the ABA was in New Orleans, and I went as Noel's assistant. This time he also allowed me to have a bit of space in his booth to show off a couple of John Daniel books and hand out our first catalog. I enjoyed New Orleans enormously, and I moved pretty independently of Noel. He did introduce me to Carolyn See and John Espey, who became friends and even authors of ours as time went by. The roller-coaster ride was there again, of course, and I bought my E Ticket.

At one point during the show I met up with Roger Moss, a fine sales rep who had sold books to me when I was at Kepler's. I gave him a copy of our catalog and showed him the few books we'd done, just to show off. Roger came back to me later (it could have been an hour later or a day later; time is slippery during the ABA) and told me that our list was too small for him and his colleagues to take us on as an independent publisher, but that he'd like to sell our books if we would agree to being distributed by Subterranean, a company he represented. He had already talked to Craig Broadley, the president of Subterranean, and had arranged for us to meet. So I met with Craig and his wife Claudia, and they explained how distribution works and how Subterranean works within that system. I came home from New Orleans with a triumph in my briefcase: we had distribution.

Subterranean was (and is) a small distributor based in Oregon. Their main client publisher is City Lights Books, and in fact they exist mainly to warehouse, sell, and fulfill for City Lights. Their other clients at that time were strange and offbeat, experimental literary presses that put out books I wouldn't want to read. I'm not sure how we fit into the mix, and our sales probably did not justify the trouble it took to have us on board, but Subterranean was good to us for a couple of years before they unloaded nearly all of their publishers in favor of concentrating just on City Lights and one or two others.

Distribution means somebody is out there selling your books, they're warehousing your books, they fill orders and accept returns, and they do the accounting and pay you on a monthly basis. They're in it for a living, of course, and it costs the publisher to be distributed. They take about thirty percent of the net receipts, for starters. They move at their own pace, which may not be very fast. They put out a catalog, which is good, but they charge you to be a part of it, which can sometimes be quite expensive. The entire time you wonder if it might not be better to be doing this stuff yourself, if only you had sales reps, warehouse space, a shipping room, an accounting system, and a lot more time.

In 1987 the ABA was back in Washington, and this year Susan and I both went. This time we shared a booth with Noel, actually putting up our own posters and putting out our own books in a handsome display. We felt like grown-ups. We had a meeting with a prospective author, Ann McLaughlin. We made a contact that ended up being our first international rights sale, Korean rights for a biography of Olympic diver Sammy Lee. We had lunch with Craig and Claudia Broadley. We worked hard and well. And we were always on the lookout for ways to improve our distribution. At that time the most prestigious distributor of small presses was Kampmann & Company, which distributed a number of literary presses including Mercury House. I'd known Eric Kampmann's brother David in Palo Alto, so I used that name to become friendly with Eric, and we shmoozed with him as much as we could without being obvious apple-polishers. We also met, because our booth was right across the aisle, Texas Monthly Press, a small publisher that was getting into the distribution game and was looking for other small presses to distribute.

When we got back to Santa Barbara, part of the follow-up work, as always, was to send notes to all the contacts we'd made at ABA. I wrote letters to Eric Kampmann and to Scott Lubeck of Texas Monthly, inviting Kampmann to distribute John Daniel books and TMP to distribute Fithian books. They both turned me down, quite nicely.

That didn't matter, because we still had Subterranean, and we were still with SubCo when we went to the 1988 ABA in Anaheim. Again we shared a booth with Capra Press. Also, because Anaheim was within driving distance (if you like to drive), we were able to go down months ahead and reserve cheap hotel rooms for us and for Noel right across the street from the convention center; we could see the tip of Disneyland's Matterhorn from our bathroom window. We were also able to shlep our samples and our display materials down to the show without having to ship them.

It was a good show for us, especially because it was a West Coast ABA, and therefore one attended by West Coast booksellers, the ones we most wanted to court. Our greatest accomplishment of that show came at the end, when Carolyn See stopped by our booth to see Noel. She was exhausted, but I persuaded her to carry off one more book in her already heavy tote bag: a bound advance proof of *Big Chocolate Cookies*, by E. S. Goldman. I had no idea at the time of the size of that accomplishment, or that it would tie in with another conversation I'd had earlier. Sometime during the show I'd spoken with Michael Siegel, from the H. N. Swanson agency. We'd swapped stories about Nancy Packer, whose name he'd noticed on our poster for her book *In My Father's House*. Michael had been a guest in one of her classes and had found her delightful.

Again, the ABA at Anaheim was a quest for greater distribution. We shmoozed with Kampmann, and with Consortium, which was the up-and-coming distinguished distributor of literary presses. Consortium had just hired a new sales manager, none other than Stephen Williamson, with whom Susan had worked at Capra a few years back. We thought we had a chance there. We also made a presentation to the Capra Press sales meeting, hoping Noel might agree to distribute our John Daniel books. Although neither Susan nor I really wanted to be working with Noel (since we'd both come out of his shop, we felt we should be doing things independently of him now as a sign of our own growth), it would have been a convenient arrangement. Also we were very fond of the Stuart Group, the family of sales reps who covered the western states for Capra and other small houses.

But Consortium turned us down and Noel turned us down. In fact, a few months later, Capra got rid of the Stuarts and all their other reps and joined Consortium.

And a few months later than that, we got a letter from Subterranean Company explaining that they were cutting back and letting us go. We were suddenly without representation and without distribution. By this time we were committed to so many projects that we simply could not afford to grow backwards. We had changed our name to John Daniel and Company, and we were putting out about ten books a year. Our books were getting well reviewed, and a couple of the titles were selling decently. We'd even sold a movie option for *Big Chocolate Cookies*. We needed a distributor.

(In the meantime, Fithian Press was doing just fine, too, with more and more authors paying to be on board. I don't mean to subordinate that part of our business to a parenthetical aside, but Fithian was not in our national distribution plans at the time, and distribution is the subject of this section.)

I called Scott Lubeck of Texas Monthly Press and reintroduced myself. He remembered me. I told him we were now looking for distribution for the John Daniel books, and he said he'd be delighted to take us on. It was so easy.

So the 1989 Washington ABA was the first time we did the show without Noel Young and Capra Press. Instead we bought a part of the Texas Monthly Booth and displayed our wares with considerable style. One of our new authors, Ann McLaughlin, lived in Washington, so we stayed at her house, and she and her husband Charlie spent a lot of time in our booth. Charlie was in a wheelchair, which made for an interesting promotional conversation piece; the novel, *Lightning in July*, was about their experience of polio. We gave away a chapbook story by Artie Shaw, to promote his short story collection, *The Best of Intentions*. We had a meeting with somebody in government (I forget which agency) to discuss the new James Bellarosa book, *A Problem of Plumbing*, a collection of stories about disability. For the first time, we did not worry about distribution. Texas Monthly was a growing company, with a bright, happy staff, and they were happy to be working with us. We counted ourselves lucky.

That luck lasted for less than a year. Sometime in the spring of 1990, dangerously close to ABA, Texas Monthly Press called us up to say they were getting out of the distribution game and were cutting us off as of that moment. Their parent company, Gulf Publishing, had made the decision. They (TMP) were as distressed as we. Gulf was even cutting them out of the book publishing business.

Because TMP was the one to break the contract, we had a pretty easy time getting terms we could accept. They paid us off promptly and shipped our books back to us at their expense and even gave us a booth at ABA (the booth they had reserved for themselves). But we were again without distribution.

As it happened, Kampmann & Company, the distributor we had courted a couple of years back, had gone bankrupt and Eric Kampmann was now the sales manager for National Book Network, a fast-growing distributor of independent presses. NBN was hungry for client publishers, Eric was hungry for whatever reward he got for bringing presses on board, and we needed distribution immediately. So, after many trying, tiring phone calls and hours spent with a tome of a contract, we signed on, just in time for ABA. By coincidence, the NBN aisle was immediately behind our booth on the ABA floor in Las Vegas.

We had many reasons to feel proud of ourselves, not the least of which was the distinguished list we were presenting, all displayed in handsome posters on "Grandmother," the huge, clunky display screen we had inherited from George Erikson when he dissolved Santa Barbara Press. At the top of the list was *Strong Drink, Strong Language,* a collection of memoirs by John Espey, an elder statesman of the L.A. literary scene; in time that book would earn us our first *New York Times* review and be shortlisted for a National Book Critics' Circle award. Next came *Rats in the Trees,* a collection of hard-hitting stories about Oakland street kids by Jess Mowry; that book won great acclaim and we eventually sold reprint rights to Viking Penguin and foreign rights here and there around the globe. Then there was *Closer to Houston,* a novel of contemporary turmoil in Central America by Stanford political scientist Richard Fagen; that one had disappointing sales but had special meaning for me because I had edited Fagen's book on Cuba when I was at the Stanford University Press. We were also justifiably proud of *Letter from Los Angeles,* poems by Charles Gullans, who hailed from the "New Formalist" school, meaning he was a former student and admirer, and admiree, of Yvor Winters; publishing that gang of poets was something we'd become known and respected for. There were other good books on the list as well, but there's no need to name them all.

It was a delightful ABA. On the floor of the convention center we worked hard, but without the desperate frenzy of trying to improve our lot. We had meetings with Eric Kampmann and Ruth Kampmann, his assistant and sister-in-law, so that we could learn the ropes and be worthy of NBN. Then in the evening we gambled and gamboled; for once the atmosphere outside the hall was even crazier than it was inside. One evening, tagging along with John Espey and Carolyn See, we celebrated at a former home of Elvis Presley, in honor of Joan Collins. Sounds tacky? Well, that's part of what ABAs are all about, and here we were in Vegas, after all. We partied like pirates.

Two for the Books

We left the ABA on Tuesday morning and drove west into the Mojave Desert, to the little town of Nipton, just inside California. The entire town consisted of a small convenience store (where people from Las Vegas came to buy California lottery tickets) and a four-room hotel that had been around since the silent picture era. We'd been told about this place by our friends and colleagues John and Cherie Rae McKinney of Olympus Press, a Santa Barbara publisher specializing in outdoor books. John and Cherie told us Nipton was restful, and that's what we wanted. And that's what we got.

The contrast between Las Vegas and Nipton was like climbing down off an out-of-control horse and into a hot bath. We booked ourselves into the Clara Bow room, stayed twenty-four hours, took walks in the desert, listened to the freight trains that rumbled and roared through almost hourly around the clock, soaked in the hot tub, and slept. When our twenty-four hours were up, we re-upped for another twenty-four.

During our forty-eight hours in Nipton, in June 1990, I wrote follow-up postcards and sent catalogs to colleagues and contacts we'd spoken with at the convention. I also made lists of things to do, based on a pocketful of notes I'd scribbled on the convention floor and at parties. This perhaps does not sound like an effective way to relax. but in fact it did relax me to sort out the genuine work from the hype, and it also let me get a handle on how much we'd accomplished.

Susan and I took stock.

Our company was on the verge of growing into a viable contender in the small-press publishing arena. We had developed a good, reliable source of income in our copublishing imprint, Fithian Press. We had earned a decent reputation for quality literary publishing under our John Daniel and Company imprint, with a distinguished stable of authors. We knew what we were doing, and we knew how to do it. We were still in our forties (in my case, just barely), and we had years ahead of us to make this business grow and succeed. At that moment, in Nipton, California in June 1990, I felt more career-related confidence and optimism than I have ever felt before or since.

We phoned Santa Barbara from Nipton and made arrangements to go forward with a step we'd been considering: to move our office from the Fithian Building on Lower State Street to the El Centro Building up near the post office, where our old friend Channing Bates hung his shingle. Stepping away from the Fithian Building was in a sense a declaration of independence from our past connections, not to mention an important change in terms of space and convenience.

We also decided to incorporate the company, and to establish a payroll. So, by the end of the summer, our new office on Canon Perdido was the corporate home of Daniel & Daniel, Publishers, Inc. We formally hired Eric Larson, who had been doing editing and typesetting work for us on a freelance basis, to become a full-time employee, our production manager. With a lawyer and an accountant, we took care of the necessary paperwork and launched a company that has kept us fed and kept us frantic ever since.

At this point I will stop this roughly chronological account of my career in small-press publishing. In the years since 1990 our company has grown considerably and has gone through many significant changes. We've had our triumphs and our blunders, and the stories have been dramatic and entertaining. We've also seen the industry change, along with American society in general, and Susan and I have changed both as people and as publishers. I've made progress in my side professions of writing and teaching. But to fill in the blanks and try to keep the memoir current would be to doom it to perpetual obsolescence, because life goes on faster than I can write.

So I stop the story in 1990. For that matter, from that point on, there's a written record of our company in the form of the minutes of our quarterly meeting of the board of directors. Each quarter I write those minutes (I'm the secretary of the corporation; Susan's president), and I add a "Publisher's Report," which tells the ongoing history of our business. These documents aren't public, and I may be the only one who will ever read them, but as a memoirist and historian I'm glad to know the story has been written.

Before closing, though, I want to reprint here a 99-word story I wrote about my fiftieth birthday. The day happens to fall on Thanksgiving, appropriately enough, and I've just finished teaching my first quarter at UCLA Extension, and an article about me has just appeared in the *Santa Barbara News Press* to celebrate the publication of *The Woman by the Bridge*, my collection of stories written over the course of twenty-five years. Susan and I will leave tomorrow morning for our annual vacation in Mexico, where we will not discuss the publishing business for two weeks.

THINGS COME TOGETHER

My fiftieth birthday is also Thanksgiving. Inside is my wife, who is also my partner in business that is also pleasure. I am relaxing, also working on a manuscript by a writer who's also a friend.

I've always dreamed I could fly. Sometimes when I dream I'm aware I'm dreaming, but it still works. As long as I know I can fly, I can fly.

On my terrace I'm unsure if I'm awake or dreaming. It doesn't matter. If I'm dreaming, Lord let me die before I wake.

As long as I know I can fly, I can fly.

CHAPTER FOUR
The Payoff

IN 1989, we were approached by Fitz Cory, a retired businessman from Santa Fe. Fitz spent time in Santa Barbara occasionally, because his mother lived in the Casa Dorinda retirement community, where a few of our authors also lived, so he'd learned about our press through local gossip. He'd also heard of us from Susan's good friend Marge Devon, the director of the Tamarind Institute in Albuquerque, and he may have heard some general publishing scuttlebutt about us because we were at that time riding a wave of modest success, having recently published our first hard-cover novel and gotten away with it (made back our expenses and then some).

Fitz Cory was a retired businessman who had spent his career in mergers and acquisitions. Now he was looking for something to do. He had decided to get into publishing. The plan he proposed was to join our company with Clear Light Publishing of Santa Fe; he would buy stock in both of our companies, and he would help run the combined business, adding his managerial experience to the mix of talent. In other words, he wanted to get back into the business of mergers and acquisitions, and then he wanted to be an executive in a publishing company.

The Payoff

The fact that Clear Light had nothing in common with John Daniel and Company did not bother Fitz. Clear Light published coffee-table photography books by Marcia Keegan about Native Americans, the Southwestern United States, and the Dalai Lama. We published literature, primarily in small paperback editions. For that matter, Fitz encouraged us to come up with a more clearly defined focus for our press, and after some brainstorming, Susan and I thought we could happily focus in literature by or for the disabled community and/or senior citizens. That idea appealed to Fitz. How that would work with a publisher of big picture books, nobody was sure.

Nevertheless, we began to have some serious talks. Fitz Cory did have business experience, and he did have capital. Susan and I wanted to grow, and we had no capital. Perhaps the details could be worked out. Perhaps we'd be willing to move to Santa Fe. Perhaps we'd be willing to work with Marcia Keegan and her husband, Harmon Houghton. Perhaps we'd be able to work with Fitz Cory.

And that's as far as we got.

Susan and I were used to working for ourselves and for each other. The idea of working for another boss wasn't acceptable. We'd done it before, and although we'd been happy at Capra Press, we were far happier on our own. Of course, Fitz Cory wasn't asking or offering to be our boss, exactly, but we could tell from all our conversations with him that he was a leader who expected to be followed. Whereas Susan and I, hand in hand, no longer followed anyone but each other.

I told this to Fitz Cory over lunch on New Year's Day, 1990. He was disappointed, but he took it well: we weren't the first publishers to turn him down. He couldn't understand it, though. Here he was, ready to sink over half a million dollars into our puny little company and guarantee us a running start on success, and we didn't want to play with him.

I think that's one of the reasons the terms "independent publishers" and "the small press" are synonymous.

What is it with us small publishers? Why are we so passionate about this profession of *mishegoss* and *tsuris*? Because believe me, in spite of the Pollyanish parable at the end of the previous chapter of this memoir, this career I've chosen is not all a magic circus ride.

For one thing, it's hard physical labor. Oh, not always. There are a lot of days and weeks when I hardly ever get off my butt, when my elbows are glued to my desk, and the heaviest object I lift is a telephone. But at any moment I may be called over to the warehouse to receive five thousand copies of a two-hundred page book. I have to take the cartons down off the truck and stack them in piles and roll the piles back to our space and restack them into mountains. At the end of almost every day I mine those mountains for cartons and individual copies to ship out that evening. There is a great deal of shlepping in my job, and books tend to be heavy. I often heard Noel Young mutter, as he lugged cartons of books up the Fithian Building steps, that in the next life he wanted to be a jeweler, so he could carry a whole year's inventory in his coat pocket. A publisher should have a strong back. Susan and I both have treacherous backs, but luckily in all our time together we've never had both backs go out at the same time. Luckily my back was strong the week I had to lift every single book in our warehouse to build pallets to be moved to another location. I conservatively estimate that weight at twenty-seven tons. Yes, literally. Since that move we've probably doubled our inventory.

Another matter is the long hours. I start each day before eight o'clock, writing up the UPS shipment to go out that day. My day ends at about seven in the evening, when Susan calls me in from the garage/shipping room, where I've been wrapping

The Payoff

packages since we got home from the office by way of the warehouse. Susan and I usually talk about work during lunch hours. I spend every Saturday at the office. I spend Sundays doing special mailings. About once a week Susan and I will spend our evening watching a rented movie while we lick stamps, fold brochures, or sticker envelopes. When we get out of town, more often than not it's to attend a bookstore signing in Los Angeles or Palo Alto, or to participate in a book fair, or to give a talk to a writers' club.

(Yes, I still like to write fiction that's not connected to the business. I do that between four-thirty and six in the morning. It's no wonder that I'm not terribly prolific.)

"At least you're working for yourself," I hear you say. "At least you're your own boss." How true. But remember that when you're working for yourself, you're also your own slave. When I told my friend Earl at Freelance Graphics that Susan and I were leaving Capra to start our own business, he congratulated me and said, "When you work for yourself you only have to work half-time—*and* you get to choose which twelve hours a day you want to work."

What else do I have to complain about? Let's talk about authors.

I don't mean writers. I'm a writer. Nothing wrong with that. We're a moody, egotistical lot, but we're fairly quiet about it, at least while we're writing. It's when writers get to be authors that a publisher must beware.

Actually writers are also a pain in the butt, whiny, sniveling, always on the make. Susan and I will have a booth at a fair, with all our current and some of our backlist books displayed, and someone will come up with a manuscript tucked under his arm. He will spend half an hour building up his courage. He will feign great interest in our publishing company by picking up book after book from our table, studying each of them carefully. After he's had enough time to memorize the back-cover copy of every book we've ever published, he reveals himself by blurting, "What kind of books do you publish?"

Okay. Okay. I feel sorry for the shnook, because I'm that shnook, too. But I sometimes think that if there were only half as many book readers as there are book writers, only half as many book purchasers as manuscript peddlers, then we small-press publishers wouldn't have such a struggle to survive.

Like a lot of kids who entered puberty a year or two behind schedule, I've been racing to catch up ever since, hoping people everywhere would like me and find me attractive. I'm like that nubbly little animal in Kipling's "Sing-Song of Old Man Kangaroo," wanting to be very much sought after. Well, eventually I found the answer: become a publisher. And eventually I found myself very much sought after, and, like Old Man Kangaroo, not liking it very much. When I go to writers' conferences to teach students how to write good fiction, or tell them how the publishing business works, they pay attention to me, and then they ask me what sort of books do I publish. I believe I know the doubts that a woman must have when a man listens to her voice but watches her cleavage.

By the way, I'm not criticizing the writing, even though most would-be writers (and many published writers) can't write for sour apples. In fact, many writers are great artists. For example, one of my oldest friends is also one of the best writers I know. But as of this writing I've lost his friendship because I turned down his 400-page contemporary novel. It is a very good book, but it doesn't fit our list, we could not afford the production, and we wouldn't be able to sell or distribute enough copies to pay for the typesetting, let alone the printing, paper, and binding. His book, which ought to make him and some New York publisher both rich, would bankrupt us. But my friend has stopped listening by now; to him I'm now the publisher who rejected him.

The Payoff

Okay, so that's writers. On to authors.

Authors want to be stars. "Why isn't my book on the front counter?" they used to ask me when I was a bookseller. Now that I'm a publisher, it's "Why isn't my book on the front counter?"

I must be fair and acknowledge that many, if not most, of our authors acknowledge the limitations of small-press publishing. We don't do best-sellers, our authors don't get invited to chat with Oprah, we're lucky to be reviewed occasionally by *Publishers Weekly*. But some of our authors, even some of the most unlikely candidates among them, the authors of memoirs even less interesting than this one, wonder why, why, why…we, the publisher, haven't done more for them. I've warned them from the start that publication at this level is its own reward, and yet they badger Susan to be a booking agent, to jump through hoops. "I'm telling you, this would be a natural for Spielberg…"

(This doesn't happen just at the small-press level. The adversarial relationship between authors and their publishers is the grist of many a cocktail-party conversation at all levels of the industry. Susan and I mix with professional writers quite a bit, and I attend writers' conferences as a speaker and workshop leader where I'm often thrown into gatherings of writers and big-name authors. Almost invariably, when two or more professional authors are gathered together, the sins of their publishers are paraded out for commiseration.)

I love our authors, I really do. But a discontented author is enough to make me want to quit the business. No wonder I've been told that my entries in the annual *Writer's Market* get crankier and crankier, year after year.

So. What else? Well, there's the overall cruelty of the book business in general and the New York Literary Establishment in particular, as long as I'm being cranky.

103

ONE FOR THE BOOKS

No, really. They're a bunch of gatekeepers, bouncers, snobs, territorial headwaiters. Our industry is like a poker game with the ante so high that only the big boys can play. You're penalized for being small. I suppose that sounds paranoid, but in fact it's just business. It's the converse of the maxim that nothing succeeds like success.

Giant chain stores like Barnes & Noble and Borders Books and Music have, for the past decade, been systematically targeting and destroying independent bookstores across this great land of ours. It's no secret, and the superstores don't apologize for it. It's the same sort of thing that's happened to mom-and-pop stores in other fields: where are the corner grocery store, druggist, and hardware shop these days? Swallowed by Safeway, Thrifty, and Builders' Emporium. Why this matters to the small publisher is that chain stores, with their streamlined, centralized, bottom-line-oriented buying, have no time for tiny publishers who won't be promoting their books on the major television networks or fronting the stores co-op advertising money. Chain stores want best-sellers, the one thing we don't provide. All we independent literary publishers know how to give them is good books, be they experimental or old-fashioned. The victims of this development in our culture have been the small bookstores, the small publishers, and the intellectual and cultural level of our society. People all across the nation laugh to exactly the same joke at exactly the same time as it's broadcast on a "Seinfeld" show (even though the joke itself was created weeks or months before), which is why practically nobody reads short stories any more. So we should get smart and do authorized biographies of "Seinfeld" stars so the chain stores will buy our wares? We can't afford to. We don't want to. And if we could get it together to publish one such book, we'd be faced with huge orders, then we'd have to take out a loan so we could go back to press to supply our big-time customers, and then, just as the newly rented warehouse space was filling up with inventory ready to ship out, the returns from the previous printing would start to come in because Random House or Simon & Schuster would have just published a bigger and flashier biography of another "Seinfeld" character, and our book would be the flavor of a week gone by.

"All you need is one best-seller," we're often told by people who don't understand our business. One best-seller would be the end of us.

A few years ago we published a collection of very entertaining memoirs by Al Capp, all centering on his having grown up with a wooden leg. The book contained a rare comic strip, an introduction by John Updike, and blurbs by Arthur Schlesinger, Al Hirshfeld, and Charles Schulz. It was reviewed favorably by *The New Yorker*, *The Atlantic*, and the *New York Times*. So how did it do? Our distributor, National Book Network, oversold it to the chain stores, and a few weeks later most of the copies were returned, slightly damaged and unsalable.

Susan and I told this story to a well-known literary publisher at a cocktail party one evening, and he chided us, saying we should have been on the phone nonstop, promoting the hell out of the book, taking advantage of all the good reviews. It was our own fault that the book flopped, because we didn't follow up. I suppose that's right, but the cost of a proper follow-up, in terms of both money and time, would have been beyond us. (And by the way, that publisher is no longer in business, and we are.)

What I wanted to happen was for the book to be hand-sold, as Susan and I used to hand-sell books to our customers when we were booksellers. I wanted bookstore clerks to say, "Hey, cool! Look, Al Capp!" But of course the clerks at B. Dalton aren't paid to hand-sell, and most of them never heard of Al Capp. ("He's that English cartoon, right? Drinks beer, plays rugby, and fights with his wife?")

So now I have trashed our major suppliers, the authors. I have trashed our major customer, the book business. It is time for me to serve up vitriol to the party in between, the publisher. My company. Myself.

Because the costliest mistakes are really nobody else's fault. If the industry sucks, I should quit whining and get out and find something I like better. If authors are hard to work with I should quit whining and get out and find people I like better to do business with. But the villain of the worst publishing nightmares is always myself, whom I can't fire.

The truth is, I love our authors. I love our business. I can pick and choose among authors, and there's always a reason for working with any particular author in spite of problems. As for the business, I may have problems with chain stores and returns, but there are ways to make a living in spite of them. But I'll never escape the speed bumps of my own imperfection.

As I've already explained, the primary source of our income is not through the sale of literature. Selling good books is important to us, but our main funding comes from selling the service of copublishing. Under our Fithian Press imprint, we copublish about forty books a year. That means we have to satisfy about forty major customers a year: we have to deliver a product that will tickle them pink. Then we have to do our very best to make sure that product (the author's book) reaches as great an audience as it can.

An author is often disappointed by the sales of his or her book. That I can't help and don't feel guilty about. We are very clear from the outset with our copublishing authors about the prospects for success in small-press publishing. If they're convinced that their books will be exceptions, they've convinced themselves in spite of my warnings. We try, but we can only do so much.

The Payoff

However, I do guarantee that the product itself will be first-class. They're paying us what it takes to keep us in business, and we owe them a book that they will be proud of. And that we will be proud of. That happens most of the time. Most of our authors feel great joy when they receive the first ten copies of their books.

But now and then we drop the ball. I drop the ball. And when that happens I go into such depression that I want to go back to working for somebody else instead. Maybe be a bookstore clerk again.

I once guaranteed an author, in writing, that her book would be bright blue. When I sent the book to press, all I remembered of that guarantee was that it was to use blue. Scrimping on costs, I used a dull, dark blue that I thought would also work well for an author photo on the back of the book (so I wouldn't have to use another press run for black). The front of the book was a dull, dark blue, not the bright blue I had guaranteed to the author. But the author's real fury was that the dull, dark blue gave her a surprise in her author's photo on the back of the book. "It makes me look like a *Negro!*" she told me. "I'm a senior citizen, and I have a very good case for a lawsuit." I let the racist remark slide by, and I wasn't worried by the lawsuit threat. The point is, I'd been forgetful and cheap, and her book wasn't the product I had guaranteed her, and so we went back to press and did the whole thing over again, costing us thousands of dollars.

Sometimes it's because I'm cheap. Sometimes forgetful or sloppy. Sometimes it's because I'm proud. I know my cover design's a great idea until the book shows up. We once had to have 2000 copies of a book rebound with a new cover because I took a chance to prove that my concept of a cover would work. We've spent many an hour in front of the television stickering over misspelled names on title pages. Inserting errata sheets. Apologies.

I am not personally responsible for every error. But I am ultimately responsible for every error. The author has no interest in hearing that it was the proofreader's fault, or the typesetter's fault, or a computer error, or a bad decision by a designer whom we hired. They pay the money to Fithian Press, an imprint of Daniel & Daniel, Publishers, Inc. They deserve their money's worth, and I deserve a big headache. It happens a couple of times a year, which is a couple of times a year too often.

The solution is to quit making mistakes, and believe me, if I could, I would. So would you.

So, as I asked only a few pages ago, why do we do it? If this job is so beset by *tsuris* and *mishegoss,* why do we persist? What's in it for us?

The answer is: plenty.

To begin with, I love working for myself, and I love it at all levels of the business. I love emptying the trash on Saturdays. Now that we have a small staff I don't get to do everything, but that's what I'd like to do: everything. I like going to the post office, answering the phones, making the coffee, making the deals, and making the books, then selling the books, then selling the subsidiary rights. Now we have Eric Larson in charge of making the books, and Carolyn Fleg goes to the post office and answers the phone, but I'm always ready to fill in when somebody doesn't show up for work.

Of course I should be writing in first person plural. Susan does half the work, at least. She does all of the accounting, and she's also the sales manager and the director of marketing. She also empties the trash when I don't get there first, and she restocks our office with supplies, including chocolate. She loves her job as much as I love mine.

The point is, we love small business. And I love being a small businessman, because my hands are on everything. Often my

The Payoff

hands are on in a controlling way; often they're on in a loving, caressing way. I'm still a graphic artist, and I love to design covers, although I also enjoy hiring a professional designer when it's appropriate. I love to write contracts. I love to edit. I love to receive shipments. Yes, I love the very heft of cartons of books, when I pile them into mountains.

I love to write back-cover copy, catalog copy, and press releases. (Back when I first moved to town and was working for Noel Young, I went to Barnaby Conrad's writers' lunch and he asked me what sort of writing I did. I told him I was a fiction writer, but for the nonce I was writing back-cover copy, catalog copy, and press releases for Capra Press. "That sounds like fiction to me," he said.) So I'm still a writer.

I love the part of my job that happens at the end of each day, because that's when I'm still a bookseller. Susan and I leave the office and go to the warehouse, where our car is parked, and we load the back of our hardworking little Honda with books to be shipped out. Then we go home, and while Susan cooks our dinner, I spend an hour or more in the garage, which is our shipping room, wrapping packages. I love Jiffy Bags. I love sealing tape. I love postage stamps and UPS tracking labels. Most of all, I love affixing an address label on the front of a package, knowing that somebody, somewhere, will receive a book that we made and will enjoy reading that book. That's when the two hands come together and I can hear applause.

And speaking of applause, one of the things I enjoy most in my job is going out as a speaker, telling classes or clubs about what happens in book publishing. That's what's left of my career as a stand-up entertainer. Speaking to rapt audiences, I hear the enthusiasm in my own voice, and I believe myself and believe in myself, no matter how much stress the past week may have handed me.

You know what else? I even enjoy that we're always under

stress, and there's never enough time to get the work done. Well, I don't love it unreservedly, but at least I can say that I haven't been bored since I moved to Santa Barbara. Not once.

Sometimes it's so hectic we nearly explode. Often we're frantically trying to solve a costly problem we've created, but there are also times when we're riding a crest of success. Like the time Ralph Nader talked about one of our books on the radio and gave out our 1-800 number and all five lines on our telephones were flashing and ringing for hours with special-order customers.

Small press publishers do it all. Yes, we rely on free-lance help, and we don't do our own printing or binding, but we're intimately involved with every book we publish, from its nine-month incubation period, through its life as it moves from the front to the middle to the back of our catalog, until it is finally remaindered to Book Heaven. This is a source of great pride and pleasure, and that's worth far more than all the high salaries and free lunches the New York houses offer to their employees.

But what do I love most about the business that I'm in? More than all the money, fame, and pride (such as they are) put together? More than my desk and the pictures stuck to my wall, more than my morning coffee, more than Eric's jokes, more than a mountain of books in the warehouse? More than Avery Labels, Jiffy Bags, Exacto Knives, and my Macintosh? More than all the independence and ideals and the art of it all?

The answer lies in what my mother first told me when I asked her what I should be when I grew up. *She told me that the people who made books were called publishers, and that publishers had to read the stories first to decide which ones to make into books.*

This is the adventure of acquisitions, an area of the business I've kept almost entirely to myself. Not true: Susan is involved in

The Payoff

every major decision, and she has acquired some of our best books, but the point is, this is my area of the business, and the one I love the most. The one without which I might quit publishing, and the one because of which I cannot.

I will tell you a few stories.

The worst mistake a publisher can make is to spell the author's name wrong on the title page. The publisher can be forgiven, though, when the author furnished him with the wrong name in the first place.

When we received a big manuscript called *Big Chocolate Cookies* by Vann Tuh, I was prepared to give it a routine once-over before returning it in the SASE provided by Frances Johnson of the Cape Cod Writers' Group. It looked like too big a project for a small West Coast publisher.

Instead, I read the first page. That compelled me to read the second page, which was even better. Within a few minutes I had gobbled the first chapter and was giving over my weekend to reading the entire manuscript, much of it aloud to Susan, following her around the house and making her drop everything from time to time, just so she could hear this magic prose.

I knew, and Susan agreed, that it was time to take a chance and publish our first full-length novel in cloth. I wrote back to Ms. Johnson, who put me in touch with Mr. E. S. Goldman, the author's friend and business manager.

Goldman and I agreed on terms that were not generous by big-time East Coast standards but were the best we could afford. I sent Vann Tuh a token advance of five hundred dollars, and *Big Chocolate Cookies* was launched. (Wrong metaphor? Went into the oven?) I began copy editing, corresponding occasionally with the author, who didn't seem to have an address of his own and who obviously borrowed E. S. Goldman's word processor for his correspondence. The editing was completed and the book was typeset, and bound galleys were produced by Crane Duplicating Service in anticipation of that year's ABA convention in Anaheim.

Meanwhile, E. S. Goldman was developing a writing career of his own. He sold three short stories to *The Atlantic*, the first of which, "The Way to the Dump," was published in December 1987. The *Boston Globe* did a story about Goldman, who, it appears, had become a fiction writer late in life, after retiring from a successful career in advertising. He was asked if he had any other irons in the fire, and he confessed that he had written a couple of novels.

By this time I was becoming suspicious. I wrote to Stanley Goldman and said, "It's *Big Chocolate Cookies* I'm interested in, no matter who wrote it. But if you and Mr. Tuh are the same person, I think we should cash in on your growing reputation."

Goldman wrote back to admit that yes, he was Vann Tuh. He also said that he now had an agent of his own, Susan P. Urstadt. "The Way to the Dump" had been selected for *Best American Short Stories of 1988*, and Urstadt now had a couple of large publishers looking at his short story collection and his other novel. She wanted to represent *Big Chocolate Cookies* as well, so although the cloth edition was spoken for, she would be selling paperback rights for the novel.

And so the short literary career of Vann Tuh came to an end. All that remained was his name on the front and back cover, spine, title page, and copyright page of several hundred bound galleys, which we repaired with crack-and-peel labels before we went to Anaheim. Luckily the book design did not call for Mr. Tuh's name on the running heads.

So that's how we acquired *Big Chocolate Cookies* and how we came to know Stanley Goldman. We handed out those bound galleys at the ABA, accompanied by a release divulging the information you've just read, and one set went to book critic Carolyn

The Payoff

See and another went to Hollywood agent Michael Siegel. When Carolyn See's review was printed in the *Los Angeles Times*, ["...an incredibly precious, goofy rigmarole of a book. It's great! It's fun! It's one of a kind!...What dialogue! What *elegance* this writer has!...This book may be hard to find, but order it if you have to. It's the BEST."] our phone began to ring like gangbusters, and within a couple of weeks we had gone back to press for a second printing and had sold a film option, thanks to Michael Siegel.

We never made much money on *Big Chocolate Cookies*, because the production costs of the reprint ate up our share of the film option money, and the sales dropped off before we'd sold many copies from the second printing. But I don't care. As a result of my reading a first page of a manuscript, our company gained in many ways, including an ongoing friendship with Stanley Goldman and with Carolyn See, and with Carolyn See's friend John Espey, whose *Strong Drink, Strong Language* we published with great success two years later. The year after that we published a memoir by Carolyn and John together called *Two Schools of Thought,* and last year we bought out a fine story collection by Goldman called *The Palmer Method*. *Big Chocolate Cookies* also brought us a working relationship with Artie Shaw, who provided a back-cover blurb; we went on to publish two books by Shaw.

As for *Big Chocolate Cookies,* it's now out of print, like many of the greatest novels ever written, and the film never got made (yet), but we can still taste the success.

The next acquisitions story again involves incomplete disclosure on the part of an author, although this time the name I'm using in the story is one that I made up. Let's call this author Elmer Dimsdale.

Several years ago, one of the local heroes in Santa Barbara

was the Humanitarian minister, a man named Elmer Dimsdale. He was a friend of Maya Angelou, he'd marched with Martin Luther King, he'd played professional football for the San Francisco Forty-Niners, and most of all he was a caring, intelligent, witty man, and a good speaker and writer, and he ran a good liberal church. Because he had such a fan club in this town, Susan and I decided to approach him and ask for a collection of his sermons to publish. We were not members of the church, but we knew people who were, and Santa Barbara is a small enough community that Dimsdale's name was well known in the philosophical circles, and ours well known in publishing circles, so it seemed a good match. Elmer agreed, and he turned over a collection, which Susan edited and we put into production. It was called *The Fine Art of Saving and Savoring the World*.

Just before the book went to press, Elmer called us up and told us he was moving to Detroit. This disturbed us because we had counted on having a local author to promote his book here in town, but Elmer persuaded us not to worry: the move would give us two markets: Santa Barbara, where he would be fondly remembered, and Detroit, where he would be a rising star. Okay, so we stuck with our original plan and ordered two thousand copies.

While the book was at the printer's we got a phone call from Detroit. Elmer wanted to give us advance notice that some embarrassing news was going to break. He'd left Santa Barbara because he'd had a couple of affairs with women in his congregation, and had felt it was best for everyone if he resigned and moved away from the situation. Now the women had come forward. Okay, Elmer. Good luck.

Well, the news broke, and it turns out not just two but dozens of women came forward, each apparently shocked to learn she wasn't the only one. The word got back to the Humanitarian headquarters and Elmer was fired from Detroit. He now works

The Payoff

in Denver as a drug counselor, and we haven't seen him since. In the meantime, all the copies of his book that we had drop shipped to Detroit came back to us, and none of the stores in Santa Barbara would carry it. We've sold about fifty copies, all to the author.

Okay, so not all acquisitions are success stories.

But that same year we did have a success story. That was the year we discovered Jess Mowry, who went on to become our biggest star. His book *Way Past Cool* was on the best-seller list in San Francisco for two months. Foreign rights were sold to publishers in Sweden, Britain, Italy, France, Germany, Japan, and who knows whereall else, and the film rights were optioned by Disney for $75,000. Paperback rights were bought by HarperCollins for $150,000, and Farrar Straus bought his next novel. Another great thing about *Way Past Cool* is that it's a great book.

But what pleases me most about *Way Past Cool*, I have to admit, is its dedication, which says (in type as large as the title on the title page): "To Susan Daniel, for taking the chance."

If this doesn't sound like small-press success to you, you're right. *Way Past Cool* was not published by us. It was published by Farrar Straus Giroux. But we still regard the book as part of our success story with Jess Mowry, because Susan and I take great pride in knowing that we "discovered" Jess Mowry. We published his first book, *Rats in the Trees* in 1990.

I don't go so far as to believe we are responsible for Jess Mowry, or that he wouldn't have made it without us. Talent as strong as his would have found its way into print and prominence eventually, and I suppose it's partly luck that let us be the first to put his voice in a book. (In fact, unbeknownst to us, Howard Junker simultaneously "discovered" Mowry for the periodical market, and published his first story in *ZYZZYVA*. *Rats in the Trees*, which contains that story, is dedicated to Junker.)

So it may have been luck, or it may have been the design of some Editor in Chief in the Sky who felt we deserved a break since we publish literature without grant funding, but I think it was Susan's sharp eye, one Sunday afternoon, that gave us the chance to work with Jess Mowry and to give him an important stepping-stone to what's come since.

The acquisitions process for other small presses may be similar to that of the major-league publishing big-time, but I doubt it. It certainly isn't for us. For one thing, we don't rely on agents to screen what we should look at; in fact we've never bought a book from an agent, and I doubt if any agent will ever sell us one, since our advances are tiny, our royalties are based on net receipts, and our print runs are minimal. The royalties don't amount to much, and an agent would have to work pretty hard for fifteen percent of almost nothing. So we have to make our own choices from scratch.

One way in which we small presses do resemble the majors is that we are loath to take chances. If a book costs us between five and ten thousand dollars to produce, we'd better be damn sure we'll win that five to ten thousand dollars back eventually, because we don't have big bucks to play with, and too many mistakes in a row would be the end of us. As a result, most of our books are by authors who have already developed a small, devoted audience. We seek out our stable of belles lettres specialists, and we pair them together with customers we've been acquiring almost as carefully over the years. In other words, we know what we're doing, most of the time, and we seldom—very seldom—gamble on something that's come in over the transom from someone we've never heard of.

And yet it happens, now and then. About once a year, from out of about five thousand manuscripts and queries that come to our post office box, we will find something irresistible. Then

The Payoff

we find ourselves reading aloud to each other, wishing we had the money, or the courage, to publish this book in spite of all odds, and then eventually realizing that *of course* we'll publish this thing and overcome the odds.

Jess Mowry's first submission to us was a whopping big novel set in Alaska, not at all the kind of book we could afford, nor the kind of book we could sell. I don't know why Susan, who got to it first, spent any time with it at all. But I'm glad she got to it first, because she recognized the presence of a writer in there. She wrote back to this unknown (we had no idea how unknown...this guy was still breaking in his first typewriter, and it was secondhand) in a way that encouraged him to try us again, and when the next manuscript, a story collection called *Rats in the Trees,* arrived, Susan read it immediately and began to say, "Don't you wish we could...?"

We couldn't, of course. We were an old-fashioned, genteel, careful press, and Jess Mowry's *Rats in the Trees* was raw and powerful and political and violent and righteous and wonderful, and of course we published it. How could we not?

Rats in the Trees was a critical success. Gary Soto, when he announced that it had won the Josephine Miles PEN/Oakland Award for Literature, called it "a fabulous debut." *Publishers Weekly* said, "Mowry's book at once saddens, overwhelms, and charms as it explores a realm unto itself—urban gangs." *Small Press* said, "Mowry makes his audience read on, not out of pity, but out of respect and fascination. The starkness of the style and the absence of condescension make these stories work and convey the newspaper headlines of 'Kid Kills Kid' in a way unlike any other."

In terms of book sales, *Rats in the Trees* was a flop. Obviously we could not peddle it to our genteel subscribers, and our distributors didn't know what to do with it either. We sold hundreds of copies, but we did not sell thousands.

Jess, however, did well. Thanks to *Rats in the Trees* and the attention it got, he started working with the Sandra Dijkstra Agency, and from there on it was the fast lane for him. He became a star, and we remained small-press publishers.

If that sounds bittersweet, I guess that's how I feel. I don't resent that we didn't get a share of the big-time money that Jess's subsequent books earned him from the New York Literary Establishment. In fact, *Rats in the Trees* eventually broke even, thanks to Sandy Dijkstra, who sold British and German rights for us, and to Mollie Friedrich, Jess's subsequent agent, who sold reprint rights to Viking Penguin.

If there's any sadness in the story, for Susan and me, it's the fact that we've had to say goodbye to Jess in a sense, as if we were sending him off to college. I know that sounds patronizing, and matronizing, and I don't have a right to feel that way, but I do. I think we'll always have a friend there, and we'll continue to get his Christmas cards, but we won't be able to work with Jess Mowry the writer again. He's outgrown us.

Such is the plight of the small-press acquisitions editor. We enjoy the discovery, then watch the glory from the grandstands.

Pete Fromm, another formerly unknown writer, sent me a collection of stories sometime in the late 1980s. I'd never heard of him, and no wonder: he'd never been published before. So, as I always do with manuscripts of short story collections, I read one story. Hey. It was good. I read another story. Even better. This man could write. His stories were real, honest, and strong. About people worth caring about. Most of them were set in the northern Rockies. They were outdoor stories about hunting and fishing and weather. They were also sensitive stories about men and women in difficult relationships. The women were as strong as the men. These were damn good stories by a damn talented writer.

The Payoff

I rejected them.

I wrote back with my sincere admiration and regret. I told him it was just too risky for us to publish a collection of short fiction by a completely unknown writer. I thanked him for the pleasure of reading his stories, wished him great luck, and advised him to start networking with as many Montana writing stars as he could—William Kittredge, Ivan Doig, Rick Bass, Jim Harrison, Richard Ford, Tom McGuane; hell I didn't know if these guys really lived in Montana or whereall, but he belonged in their company—and told him to submit the stories to literary quarterlies. If he could only develop a track record and an audience, I knew he'd have a future.

Pete Fromm took my advice. Actually, he was smart enough to be doing all that already, without my advice. In any case, the next time he wrote to me, a couple of years later, he had a list of several publication credits, including some of the stories I'd already read. And he dropped Bill Kittredge's name.

I got on the phone and asked Joyce Abdill, our sales rep in the Pacific Northwest, whether or not she felt he-man Montana fiction was still a hot genre, and she said definitely. So I wrote to Pete Fromm and said I'd publish a book of his if it could be built around a northern Rockies theme. He sent me *The Tall Uncut,* and we were committed.

That book has now had three printings, and Pete has since gone on and published subsequent books with Lyons & Burford, St. Martin's Press, Stackpole Books, and Scholastic Publishing Company. I deserve none of the credit for Pete Fromm's success, but I claim my share anyway, along with ten percent of whatever he may earn on future rights to *The Tall Uncut.*

More important to me than the credit or than the tithe is the friendship I have with Pete, a literary friendship that means we swap our short stories for critique and console each other with war stories about the way we're treated by publishers and agents. I have visited him in Great Falls, and he has visited me in Santa Barbara. We have drunk beer together. Yes, I know this sounds like the winner of the annual Bad Hemingway contest. I will buy a copy of every book that Pete Fromm publishes, and he will always remember that I bought the right to publish his first book. And it was a good book. It was a clean, well-lighted book.

When Barnaby Conrad and Shelly Lowenkopf took me to lunch five years ago and invited me to join the faculty of the Santa Barbara Writers' Conference, I was honored and delighted, and I accepted quickly. I had only one reservation, but it was an easy one to dismiss for the moment. The main thing is I love fiction, I enjoy teaching, and I like the company of fellow writers who take their craft seriously. I've participated as a teacher or workshop leader in several conferences, large and small, and I've always enjoyed the experience except for one minor annoyance.

So I accepted the position with a proud smile.

Then Shelly said, "Who knows? You're a publisher and there are lots of good writers who come to the conference. You might find a book to publish."

Tilt.

That was my one reservation. My observation has been that writers attend writing conferences for two reasons: to work on their craft and to work on their careers. The craft part I love. The career part makes me very uncomfortable. And so when I participate in conferences and workshops I find myself politely dodging would-be authors, hoping they're not interested in me simply because of what I can do for their careers. And as eager as I was to join the prestigious faculty of the Santa Barbara Writers' Conference, I worried that I'd find myself in the awkward position of avoiding and disappointing hopeful writers in my own home town.

The Payoff

I needn't have worried. My class was the swing shift, from nine-thirty till the wee hours of the morning, when the only writers still awake are serious writers who are devoted to getting their words in order. It has turned out to be one of the highlights of my year. I, who naturally rise early and retire early, find myself wired by coffee and adrenaline and loving every late-night hour of that conference week. And nobody, or practically nobody, hits on me for the wrong reason.

And yet, the joke's on me. My very first night at the Writers Conference I sat in on Shelly's workshop to see how he led it. That was my training session, after which I'd be on my own. The very first person to get up and read was a woman named Yvonne Nelson Perry, and she read a short, powerful story set in Hawaii. A very powerful story indeed. The next night Yvonne came to my workshop and read another very short, very powerful story, also set in Hawaii. Next night, same thing. By the end of my first week at the Santa Barbara Writers Conference, I had heard most of what I now knew was a story collection in progress, all stories about the real people of the non-touristy Hawaii. *The Other Side of the Island.* Stories about death, love, work, choice, change, challenge, danger, laughter, violence, language, races, glory, people, people, people.

I was hooked. After the conference was over I wrote to Yvonne Nelson Perry and begged her to let me publish her book.

The book has done well. It hasn't sold like hotcakes, but it's done well in Hawaii, thanks to a connection I made at ABA with a Hawaiian distributor. It also sells to Yvonne, who takes her books to writers' conferences, because she's now a teacher and workshop leader too. One of the reasons she's become a successful workshop leader on the writers' conference circuit is that she has a published book. Thanks to John Daniel and Company.

In the summer of 1987, Susan and I were honeymooning in San

Luis Obispo, when we came across a copy of the *New Times*, the free weekly paper of that town, in which was announced a brand new annual contest called 55 Fiction. There were a lot of complicated rules, but they boiled down to this: each entry had to be a complete short story, with plot, setting, and character, within fifty-five words. Great gimmick, I thought, and thought no more about it.

A few weeks later, back in Santa Barbara, I found myself unable to sleep one hot full-moon Santa Ana night, so I got out of bed, dressed, and took a walk around the neighborhood. As I walked, I mulled over a story plot I had made up some thirty years ago and never done anything with. There and then I decided to write the story, and since it was to be only fifty-five words, I figured I could make it up as I walked, before I returned to my bed and went to sleep. Which I did. It took me about fifteen minutes.

In the morning I carried my story, in my head, to the office and keyed it into MacWrite. That took me about five minutes. I counted the words and saw that I had written 237. It took me over two hours to pare down the story into fifty-five words. I sent the story off to the *New Times* and thought no more about it until a friend in San Luis Obispo called me to congratulate me because I had won first prize.

You can imagine how thrilled I was. There was no money involved, but I won a tee shirt and a certificate, and my words in print, and the accomplishment—not of having won a prize, but having finally gotten that thirty-year-old story into words.

Since that time, I have recycled the story, "Guitar," several times. I managed to get it reprinted in *Publishers Weekly*, I included it in my published volume of short stories (*The Woman by the Bridge*, Dolphin Moon Press), and my son Morgan in Mendocino used it briefly as his answering machine message. I daresay more people know my writing from those fifty-five

The Payoff

words than from any other words I've ever written under my own name.

But that was only the beginning.

In the spring of 1994, Steve Moss, editor of the *New Times*, came to Santa Barbara to meet with Susan and me to get some advice on how to go about publishing a collection of the best fifty-five-word stories published in the newspaper over the past eight years. We found Steve to be a delightful person, and the book project he showed us was really exciting. We gave him all kinds of valuable advice and sent him on his way, envying him for having such a clever idea and such an entertainment-packed book to publish.

We began plotting. Acquiring.

A few phone calls later, and we were on board. We ended up publishing *The World's Shortest Stories* in conjunction with New Times Press. They did all the design and production, and our job was marketing, promotion, sales, distribution, and a bunch of busywork details connected with book publishing.

The book has been one of our biggest hits. We started with five thousand copies and we've gone back to press twice. And, thanks to an introduction provided by my old friend Craig McCroskey of Book Travelers West, we've now sold reprint rights for the book to Running Press.

These stories go on and on, but there's only so much a reader will take, and so I'll stop here. I only want to say that of all the intoxicating rewards that small-press publishing has given me, and there have been plenty, there's no joy so strong as that of discovery, development, and release, watching something beautiful happen just because I was smart enough to say yes at the right time.

You see: I do love authors after all.

And I love my job.

And I believe I'm the first person ever to write about being a literary editor without once mentioning Maxwell Perkins by name. Oops.

Every now and then some article will call the small-press movement new, labeling it a revolutionary answer to the big-time, major-league, New York publishing establishment. This maxim has been spouted repeatedly as long as I've been around publishing, which goes back to the course I took at Radcliffe in the summer of 1964.

It's baloney. The fact is small-press publishing is not new at all. It's older than large publishing and it's older than New York. It began with Gutenberg and the invention of movable type, over five hundred years ago. Of course almost nobody uses the same technology anymore (movable type? what's that?), but other traditions remain: small presses today are companies with small staffs, doing books in small editions, with a lot of loving care, just like Gutenberg.

The history of publishing in the United States is also grounded in the small press, with writers who became printers and then sold their product on pushcarts. Eventually these writer/printer/booksellers began trading their wares and turned into authors, publishers, and bookstores, the modern-day overgrown descendants of which are Stephen King, Random House, and Barnes & Noble.

But in the meantime, the small presses have continued throughout our history, and thanks to their courage we have the works of such American writers as Thomas Paine, Herman Melville, Walt Whitman, Edgar Allan Poe, Anaïs Nin, Yvor Winters, Charles Bukowski, Raymond Carver, and Jess Mowry, to name just a very few, all of whose careers were launched by small, independent houses.

The Payoff

There may be something very beautiful about things large and fast. But I have greater affection for all things small and slow. Thoreau said books should be read slowly and carefully, as they were written. As they were written, so should they be published.